MEDITATION
FOR HEALING!

MEDITATION FOR HEALING

by Justin F. Stone

Great numbers of men and women are interested in the practice of meditation for health benefits, but how many of them know that there are many types of meditation, each causing a different effect in the meditator? *Meditation for Healing* offers detailed instruction in different kinds of meditation, elaborates on the physical and mental results to be experienced, and discusses the background and underlying philosophy of each.

With the spreading interest in alternative forms of self-healing, such a book seems a *must* for those who wish to suggest meditation as a healing force to patients or friends. Doctors, psychologists, educators, and all readers will find this a valuable text and do-it-yourself guide to meditational healing. The methods taught in *Meditation for Healing* may very well indicate the direction of healing arts in the future.

About the Author

Justin F. Stone studied many years in Japan, China, and India, and later taught Oriental Philosophy, T'ai Chi Ch'uan, T'ai Chi Chih, and Comparative Meditation at universities in the United States. He is the author of a number of metaphysical books, plus a "rapid English" language method. He is the originator of the powerful moving meditation known as T'ai Chi Chih! Joy thru Movement, of which there are now over 1100 accredited teachers worldwide. Stone is a former advisor and allied member of the New York Stock Exchange, and is a composer-member of ASCAP. Active in composing, writing, teaching, and painting in his early eighties, Justin Stone makes his home in Albuquerque, New Mexico where several shows of his paintings have taken place.

MEDITATION
FOR
HEALING

by
Justin F. Stone

Good Karma Publishing, Inc.
P.O. Box 511
Fort Yates, ND 58538

GOOD KARMA PUBLISHING, Inc.
202 Main Street
P.O. Box 511
Fort Yates, ND 58538

Printed in the United States of America by Sheridan Books, Chelsea, MI

First Good Karma Publishing, Inc. edition - 1993
Second Printing - 1995
Third Printing - 1997
Fourth Printing - 2001

Photographs on pp. 124-128 & 130 - Kimberly Grant
All other photographs, including cover photo - personal collection of Justin F. Stone
Used with permission

♻ *Text printed on recycled paper*

Library of Congress Catalog Card Number 95-75956

ISBN 1-882290-00-3

TABLE OF CONTENTS

*Dedicated to all those
who suffer, in the fond hope that
this book may help lessen their
suffering.*

MEDITATION
UNCOVERS
JOY!
AND *JOY* IS THE GREATEST HEALER

AT THE CENTER OF OUR BEING IS JOY; ALL WE HAVE TO DO IS ALLOW IT TO SHINE THRU.

The author in 1969 at a sacred
Tenrikyo Ceremony in Nara, Japan

The author in
1976 at the age of 60

FOREWORD

The increasing momentum for the actualization of Holistic ideals and practices in all areas of life including medicine and health, reflects the wide-spread reawakening awareness that to be a human being means to be at one with all aspects of one's being. Problems, dis-eases and disharmonies do not occur in a vacuum unrelated to the events, attitudes, thoughts, feelings and activities forming the total environment in which they occur. To be holistic is to realize and experience that mind, body, and spirit are so inter-related as to truly be one. To be holistic is also to be meditative.

Meditation for Healing is a holistic work in many important ways. Justin Stone is responsible for every aspect of the book's creation including not only its style and content, but also its arrangement and compilation and its design and format. Like all of Justin's works, this material derives from his great personal experience with the various meditative practices outlined. Studying with great teachers and masters, practicing rigorously, developing and creating new techniques, and teaching many students over the years has given Justin a rich glow reflecting his inner unity. Justin's writing style is a blend of descriptive and easily understandable phrases with personal anecdotes and revelations. This style indicates Justin's attention to radiating outward to his readers and inward to his center and shaping the two as one. The great variety of practices discussed and instructions revealed, again reflects knowledge of the varied needs different personalities have in regard to meditative techniques and goals. At the same time it is clear that despite the variety of practices used to achieve differing ends, healing simply occurs or health simply exists when the total and pure state of absolute meditation exists. If this state is reached, irrespective of any conceptual opinion about it, healing takes place. Justin addresses this point in the introduction to the book when he says "When Meditation achieves Total Abstraction, for the moment there is complete healing. This passes as the abstraction fades, but it has had its effect."

Meditation and health both are holistic ways of being with Self and Existence. Neither can be just read about or thought about or talked about to be experienced. To the extent that one can find one, or more, of the practices in this book which fits and resonates well with one's being, and to the extent that one practices regularly, this book will certainly be a most creative and valuable tool in living well and being in good health throughout a lifetime.

Harold A. Cohen, M.D.

INTRODUCTION

The author's interest in "healing" thru "spiritual" means goes back many, many years. Such healing methods must stand the test of actual practice; results must be achieved. Simply to believe in something because one *wants* it to be true is delusion, and delusion is diametrically opposed to true spirituality.

One hears of such healing practices as "aura adjustment," though there is nothing in the teachings of any of the great masters of the Orient about such. People speak of "astral," the "etheric body" and other concepts, in regard to healing, as though they have actually experienced them rather than merely having read about them. Twenty five hundred years ago the Buddha cautioned against believing what had not been experienced; his teaching was aimed at pointing the way for followers to arrive at the same states he had known and to have the enlightenment experience for themselves. Today, such a spiritual iconoclast as Krishnamurti says: "Don't believe it because somebody else tells you to!" This is reinforced by the Chinese saying: "You cannot appease your hunger by reading a menu." This is healthy skepticism. If the reader wants to experience the healing practices in this book, he will have to perform them regularly for himself; mere belief in them will avail nothing.

Nevertheless, the author has seen and experienced

remarkable results thru various practices of meditation. Many years of work with the Japanese "Healing Church," Sekai Kyu Seikyo, brought him to an understanding of what illness really is and how the body and the psyche are related. He saw many interesting results, not only with humans, but with plants; the same life force flows thru all living things. From this came an understanding that illness, misfortune and misery all have a spiritual basis. The Healing Church speaks of illness as "purification"; in many cases, for instance, fever is to be welcomed as it melts "accumulated toxin" and, after some suffering with it, enables the physical organism to purify itself. The author saw how this caused such chronic and unpleasant maladies as Herpes Simplex, where the heat of the sun's rays take the place of fever in melting the accumulated toxin. To suppress such manifestation because it is unpleasant cosmetically will only increase the state of dis-ease and require a new purification of greater intensity.

In the late 1950's, the author, who had always been fascinated by Chinese lore, was first exposed to T'ai Chi Ch'uan and Taoist teachings. Fascination with Chinese health methods based on an understanding of the Cosmos, not just physiology, and realization that Chinese medicine was thousands of years older than Western symptomatic medicine led the author to seek Chinese sages and scholars who could teach some of the great wisdom of the Yin-Yang system. Such men as Professor Wen-shan Huang, Dr. Chung-yuan Chang, Tin Chin Lee, Professor Nan, Dr. Wu, and the patriarch Liu all contributed to the author's study, and outlined paths of practice to be followed. Particularly there is gratitude to Professor Huang, anthropologist, culturologist, scholar, T'ai Chi master, and philosopher — a true Buddhist-Taoist-Confucianist in the great Chinese tradition. The Chinese are very practical people, and there is much to be learned by studying their ancient teachings.

In India it is believed that all illness is the result of an imbalance of the "Prana" (intrinsic energy of the individual, being merely a part of the universal energy that the Indians also know, and sometimes worship, as Shakti and Kundalini). Indian philosophy says that, in the final analysis, there is only space (Akasha) and energy (Prana) in this manifested universe. Science tends to corroborate this view, hence the theories of atomic energy, where "matter" now turns out to be energy. Oriental teaching goes farther, however, and says that, ultimately, this energy is of the nature of thought.

A mastery of this Prana energy in its individual and universal aspects would be the greatest power, capable of creating universes. Conversely, dissipation and imbalance of the Prana lead to illness and unhappy lives. To fully understand this point of view, one must stop thinking dualistically and understand all life as being part of one continuum.

Naturally, ancient Ayurvedic medicine of India sought to heal the imbalance of Prana when it appeared, through use of herbs and more esoteric ways of setting up counter-vibrations. Use of mantra, changing the vibration (and Prana through vibration) was much the goal of medicine as it was of yoga. Both wished to take the fragmented and make it whole.

Similarly, in China, illness is looked upon as a radical imbalance between the Yang (positive) Chi and Yin (negative) Chi — and "Chi" is simply the Chinese name for Prana.

In Chinese cosmology, from the ineffable Reality, originally we get a manifestation of two forces, Yang (heat, light, expansion, male) and Yin (cold, dark, contracting, female), thus setting up the first polarity. It is the juxtaposition of these two forces, and imbalance of them, that brings the world into being — creating heaven, earth and man. Man is the result of the "wedding" of the great Yang (heaven) and the great Yin (earth), which are represented in the body by the heart (Yang) and the kidneys (Yin). From these proceed the world of the 10,000 things; the endless phenomena of life.

When the Chi that flows in the individual, and creates the individual, is radically out of balance, Chinese medicine (acupuncture) tries to bring them back into balance. This is Total Organism medicine, not bothering with local symptoms except as signposts on the way. This medicine is very old, and we can see how it agrees with ancient Indian healing methods in trying to restore balance — whether we call it "vibratory balance" or use such expressions as "balancing the polarity" (Yin and Yang).

This being so, how does meditation fit into the picture? In what way is it curative? To answer this we must quote briefly from a Chinese source:

"The reciprocal character of Mind and Prana means that a certain type of mind, or mental activity, is invariably accompanied by a corresponding character and rhythm, which is reflected in the phenomenon of breathing (the first manifestation of the Vital Force, and often associated with Prana, as in Pranayama or breathing practices). Thus anger produces not only an inflamed thought-feeling, but also a harsh and accentuated roughness of breath. On the other hand, calm concentration brings the breathing to a very subtle and almost imperceptible level."

It is no wonder that the Buddha said: "When the body is mastered, the mind is mastered — and vice-versa."

The reciprocal character of mind and energy means that we can reach one thru the other. This is why such great mental serenity seems to be achieved thru the moving meditations, T'ai Chi Chih and T'ai Chi Ch'uan, which are essentially physical, and which directly circulate and balance the intrinsic energy (Chi).

Taking the above into consideration, we can see how a disturbed mind causes "inflamed" breathing and unbalanced Chi. Conversely, deep and one-pointed concentration and meditation reintegrate the mind, bringing it to a focus, with similar integration of the Yin-Yang elements of the Chi energy.

When we study Chinese cosmology deeply and learn the influence of the seasons, the elements, the times of day, we begin to intuit how the flow of the Chi varies, and how we are affected by it. These Chinese masters know where the Chi is flowing strongly in the body at any time, relative to the time of day, the season of the year, and other influences. From nine external pulses, the Chinese acupuncturist can discern imbalance in the vital force of the internal organs. He is not interested in a localized pain or discomfort; his aim is to restore balance of the over-all life force.

In observing healing work thruout the Orient, either consciously carried out or thru religious services and Yoga-like practices, the author has noted the unifying principle in them all, that is, bringing the Chi into balance and reintegrating the individual. Perhaps in other cultures "witch doctors" and "medicine men" try to do the same thing.

When after many, many years of study the author began to develop the moving meditation "T'ai Chi Chih", he realized he was working with this basic life force, the Chi. And when, in its incipient stages, he used T'ai Chi Chih mentally to augment the healing practice known as "Johrei" in the Japanese Healing Church, he got results far beyond any that he had contemplated. So strong were the results of the combined forces that he eventually gave up doing the healing work. In the final analysis, the best *healing* is *self-healing*, and there is no better way to achieve this than thru the various types of meditative practice.

When meditation achieves Total Abstraction, for the moment there is complete healing. This passes as the abstraction fades, but it has had its effect. In such meditations as the Nei Kung, the Reverse Meditative Breathings, and the Moving Meditations we work directly with Chi itself. Results have been amazing; seemingly "incurable" chronic ailments such as heart trouble, asthma, high blood pressure, even diabetes, seem to yield to the radical change in Chi balance. Such results are not promised; each must seek for himself. The author has seen many of these results and there are others documented by handwritten letters he has received

So we can begin to study meditation and the way it affects the Pranic balance and, while studying and practicing, perhaps gain the benefits of meditation the way so many others have. All it takes is perseverence.

Drawing by Justin F. Stone

Chapter 1
MANY MEDITATIONS
— MANY EFFECTS

Meditation is a healing force. It enables the meditator to harmonize his outer life with the deepest levels of consciousness, to probe the unknown levels of the subconscious and to express, or manifest, the Joy and Vital Force that are inseparable from his being.

There are numerous forms of meditation, and there are related practices — such as Japa (repetition of a name of God) or remembrance of the Buddha — that start as concentration and, at deeper levels, become true meditation. When the roving, fragmented mind is silenced and becomes one-pointed in concentration, we go far beyond disturbing thoughts and, leaving the little ego-identity behind, we reach the Source of our Being, whatever we may choose to call it. We then understand the meaning of the phrase "The Kingdom of Heaven is Within," and find it is no idle statement.

There are moving meditations and there is chanting in which the practicer can lose himself. All these aim at bringing the mind to a point. The scattered mind is weak; the integrated mind is strong in the same sense that the sun's rays, magnified, burn up almost anything. The fully concentrated mind that has reached absolute steadiness in the state of Samadhi (highest level of meditation, the end result known as the "superconscious state") can burn away all afflictions and habit tendencies. The powers of one who lives continually with concentrated mind are enormous. They are sometimes thought of as miraculous, but things are only supernatural when we do not understand the causes. To a native in a jungle, the sound of a loudspeaker blaring out words in his own tongue from a plane overhead could only be interpreted as a "miraculous voice" from the sky. Those who are familiar with airplanes and electronic equipment know otherwise.

All effects proceed from causes. When we plant the proper seeds, and nurture them faithfully, we can harvest the desired fruit. It is as simple as that. Repetition of constructive patterns brings about beneficial habit energies (known as Vashanas) in the mind, in the same way that continued practice does for the hands of the skilled pianist. These habit energies become part of our nature; indeed, they form our nature. We are the product of the seeds we have planted in the past, and our future will be the result of the seeds we are planting now. We can do nothing to undo the past, but we can determine the present and thus shape the future. Nothing happens by accident. When we understand this, and take the responsibility for our own lives, we begin to realize we can plant any seeds we desire, and get any desired effect if we are willing to pay the price, such as continued practice of meditation.

In India it is believed that intense meditation "burns the seeds of Karma," that is, erases the "sins" we have committed and nullifies the effects by doing away with the habit energies and tendencies they have created. Take the match away from the arsonist and he cannot set a fire. Purify the mind of the negative traits that have developed, thru meditative practice leading to pure consciousness, and there will be no results from these negative character-istics. The unsullied mind is the "Pure Land" spoken of in the cult of Amitabha, the Buddha of Infinite Light.

The sacred Gayatri Mantra is said to absolve all sins. Whether this is true or not, one who meditates regularly with this popular formula will find the fears of retribution disappearing, thus certainly contributing to better health and lessening of tensions on a subconscious level. There is no doubt we can remake ourselves by regular intensive concentration and meditation.

Different forms of meditation cause different effects — physically, mentally, and psychically. Chinese meditation tends to be physically healing and energizing, most Indian meditation is "other-worldly" and leads to euphoric trance, Zen meditation brings greater awareness, and Tibetan types which are far too complex for the busy person have, as the first goal, the production of the inner heat, known as the "Dumo Heat," that is said to be the basis of all Tibetan magic play. Comparatively simple forms of meditation, easy to learn and easy to practice, will bring results in terms of better health and great spiritual benefits. The non-believer will derive these benefits as well as the believer, and the religious person will find his faith in his own religion deepened and strengthened.

Today we hear of holistic institutes using many means of self-culture, with meditation as one of the pillars of practice. Many medical doctors are recommending meditation to their patients, believing that the surcease of tension brought about by regular meditation can very definitely relieve or cure illness. Such efforts are to be applauded, but the problem is that most doctors have had little experience with meditation. Perhaps they mistakenly feel there is only "meditation" and do not know there are many varied types, each causing different effects. It is one of the aims of this book to acquaint them — and others — with the techniques of many types of meditation, with explanation of the background of each and the possible benefits to be expected. When we enter an ice cream parlor, we may find 31 flavors to choose from, and we pick the one that is most appealing to our palate. A woman does not just buy a "dress" — she chooses a particular size, color, and style. By being exposed to a wide range of possible meditative techniques, the aspirant will be offered the opportunity to choose what is best for him, individually — not what his friends do, or what is most publicized. This may ultimately save time, spare disillusionment, and even save money.

The importance of choosing the appropriate meditation (and, indeed, the fitting spiritual practice, if such is desired) cannot be over emphasized. There is the case of a great professional football player, a quarterback, who has been publicized as doing Mantra meditation in the locker room just before the start of his Sunday afternoon game. One comes out of such deep immersion with a floating, euphoric feeling, and all great teachers have cautioned that the meditator should rest and remain inactive for a period after meditation. The mind, having become one-pointed and blissful, does not want to become outgoing and fragmented again. It is usually in an other-worldly state hardly compatible with going into violent action against ferocious charging 260 pound linemen on the opposing team! It is hardly surprising that this great player, admittedly on a weak team, is having bad seasons.

To further illustrate: At one time in Kyoto, Japan, the author was teaching a class at a nearby language school early in the morning, then, after an hour's interval, instructing a class of ministers at the Tenrikyo Kotoku Church community where he was living. During that one hour interval, the author was doing deep Mantra meditation in his room right up to the time of the next class. Much to his own amazement, he found himself cranky and disagreeable in the class, biting the heads off people he liked very much. This seemed so strange to him that he gave it considerable thought, and decided to curtail his deep meditation period to a half hour, and then quietly sit drinking tea while the deep meditative immersion gradually faded. The result was as expected; he regained his amiability and no longer made class hellish for his patient minister pupils.

At the end of one Comparative Meditation course which the author was giving in New Mexico, during which seven or eight meditative techniques had been taught and practiced, one student, a tall young man of about thirty, stood up and said: "I like quite a few of the techniques, especially the Mantra and T'ien T'ai ones. Which do you advise me to concentrate on?"

"What kind of work do you do?" he was asked, in reply.

"I'm a race-car driver!" was the surprising answer.

"In that case, if you're going to do Mantra meditation before races, you'll probably crack up in the first thousand yards! There is great spiritual benefit in all kinds of Japa (repetition of Mantras), but what you want is something that will place you squarely in the present and increase your awareness. The T'ien T'ai will do that, Zen meditation will do that, and the Buddha's Satipatthana certainly will do it. If you want to add to one of these the Nei Kung technique before going to sleep, you will probably develop great energy and alertness, which should stand you in good stead."

There are two basic reasons why people come to meditation, and sometimes they overlap.

First, there are those who take up meditation to gain

physical benefits, relief from chronic illness, or surcease from the pressures of our society. In China, over the years, many books have been written describing the recovery some very sick person had made due to Taoist, Tibetan, Zen, or T'ien T'ai meditation. These generally had few, if any, references to spiritual benefits and were mostly instruction for physical culture thru meditation. Those who take up meditation for their health may also expect some increase in their mental capacity, such as in memory. They may also unexpectedly obtain an intimation of deeper spiritual levels of which they had not been aware. Regular meditation is an excellent way to improve health, gain energy, and raise an individual's performance potential. It is best, however, that those who meditate for long periods of time offset the quiet inactivity with something that will again cause the vital force (Prana, Chi) to flow; otherwise there may be illness. T'ai Chi practice (moving meditation), as well as true Hatha Yoga, are effective in renewing this flow of the intrinsic energy. This secret seems to have been nearly forgotten in Japan. The author has never met a Japanese monk who did not suffer stomach trouble, probably due to the long hours of unrelieved quiet sitting (sometimes directly after meals) and the poor food, usually without roughage, that is the standard fare at Zen temples.

The second type of person who comes to meditation is one who is seeking Ultimate Answers. Whether we call this a religious quest or not, he or she is usually driven by the necessity of probing deeper and deeper into the meaning of life and, particularly, death. Some Zen temples have a placque in front which reads: "Only those vitally concerned with the problem of Life and Death have any business here."

Orientals would say these seekers are continuing on a path they had begun to follow in other lives. When such a search becomes all consuming, one leaves the world and becomes a Sanyasin (renunciate) in India or a monk in Japan, China, Korea, or Tibet. Meditation — and accompanying studies and practices — becomes a way of life. Meditation is not just another activity to such seekers, it is the ridgepole center of living. In classic Rajah Yoga, the Yogi goes thru five outer disciplines (conduct and attitude, plus Yoga postures, breathing practices, and withdrawal of the senses from their fields of activity) in order to arrive at the triple discipline of concentration, meditation, and the super-conscious state resulting from deepest meditation.

The word "Zen" literally means meditation, and the Zen sect is known as the "Meditation Sect" of Buddhism. Sufi aspirants and adepts, Taoist practicers, and Tantriks also make various forms of meditation the keystone of their varied ways. Almost all forms of Yoga depend on meditation. Indeed, the definition of Yoga by the "Father of Yoga", the Indian Patanjali — "Inhibition or Cessation of Mental Modifications" — is also a perfect definition of deep meditation.

These mental modifications of everyday life are what make us what we are. Not only do they form the seeds of Karma from which we gain the fruits — pleasing or unpleasing, in what we mistakenly think of as fate — but any change in our way of thinking and the habit tendencies thereof will greatly affect our health, change our personality, and color our attitude toward life. It would really not be too much to say that our mental habit energies are responsible for making this world a paradise or its opposite for us.

"If you don't like the world, change yourself," advised the Buddha 2500 years ago, thus dooming to disappointment the "do-gooders" who want to bring peace and serenity to the world without experiencing it themselves. This is a message of great hope. It means your future will coincide exactly with the seeds you plant now. There is nothing to do about the past; it is dead and gone, though its effects are felt in the present. If you want an apple tree in the future, all you have to do is plant some apple seeds — you certainly won't get lemons!

Meditation is the surest way to change the focus of the mind and to build the new habit energies that will bring the fruit we wish to pick. It is deepest meditation that undoes the damage that has been done, both in the body and the mind, which are not separate but a continuum in which each is conditioned by the other.

If you wish "healing" thru meditation, all you have to do is to learn the appropriate meditative technique and practice it regularly. Until now it has been the custom to follow one teacher and do the form of meditation he teaches, without becoming familiar with other types. This is a hit-or-miss method that depends largely on coincidence; you take up one form or another because a friend does it or because you hear a lecture extolling its merits; perhaps someone sells you a bill of goods with great promises of what *his* guru's meditation will do for you. You may even pay a large sum of money to be initiated with a Mantra, not by the master himself, but by an ordinary human who has been delegated to perform such a ceremony. This is somewhat dubious in nature, and there is the chance that you will wind up practicing devotion to Japanese Shinto gods or to Hindu deities with Sanskrit names without knowing that you are doing so.

Some years ago, in answer to this problem, the author began teaching his concept, "Comparative Meditation," at the University of New Mexico and elsewhere. The results were gratifying. Students would faithfully practice the different forms of meditation, one by one. In the end, each made his choice according to his individual propensities. Those willing to sit for long periods of time in uncomfortable cross-legged pose, to undergo strict discipline, and to perhaps grapple with the mind-breaking Koan (insoluble problem), would often choose Zen meditation, known as Zazen. Not too many are equipped for this difficult training involving mind and body control, however. Mantra meditation, where the special phrase takes over and leads the meditator down an effortless path, is more apt to appeal to most. It must be noted, however, that there are many techniques of Mantra meditation, as will been seen later in this book. And there are unsuspected dangers involved in this form of meditation when it becomes too passive. Astral traveling, and even obsession from without, are possibilities if one practices them incorrectly.

For those who do not wish to use names of divinity, the "Breath Dhyana" will obtain exactly the same result, namely the erasure of thoughts and a period of rest in a state of pure unmodified consciousness. Sometimes the choices students make are surprising. Unexpected traits are uncovered when students meditate, and often they discover depths and tendencies they had not previously expected. As one lawyer put it: "Suddenly I discover I'm a religious person!"

There is a division of opinion in the Orient as to whether the practicer has to know something about the discipline he practices. For instance, Japanese Zen monks chant in a transliteration of the Sanskrit that comes out as a mixture of Chinese and Japanese. After a while the words just become meaningless sounds. When an American Zen teacher changed things so Americans were chanting in English, his master is said to have broken relations with him. Admittedly, the Chinese/Japanese was not the original language and there is nothing "holy" about it. Here tradition plays a great role, and questioning is not encouraged. However, the author believes, for the Western mind, it is imperative to explain and to teach some of the background of the meditative discipline the student is to do so that he will not be working with something basically repelling to him. This is the reason for the explanation thruout this book. It is hoped that such explanation will be helpful to the reader in determining what discipline he wishes to follow. Certainly it should make it easier for the doctor, psychologist, and educator to determine what types of meditation he will recommend. Meditation is healing and spiritually edifying. The more that is known about it, the more motivated one will be to try it. The purpose of this book is to make known more about meditation, stressing the healing benefits that can be achieved. It is hoped that great benefits result from the practices taught in its pages. Meditation for healing is certainly a reality.

Chapter 2
WHAT IS MEDITATION?

So far we have talked mostly about the effects of meditation. Now it is time to ask the question: "What is meditation and how does it work?"

"A candle does not flicker in a windless spot." This is a description of the state of mind when there are no disturbances to alter its innate brilliance and steadiness. It is the same as saying: "When the wind subsides, there are no waves and the surface of the water is smooth and serene."

How do we reach such a state? We have been told by teachers that the mind is complete, that it contains all wisdom latent within it, but how do we uncover the "dust" that has gathered and obscured the natural brilliance of the mind? For this we use meditation techniques with the firm conviction that in time we will reach the serene state described by the Chinese monk-poet in the following poem:

I gather Chrysanthemums at the Eastern hedgerow
And silently gaze at the Southern mountains.
The mountain air is beautiful in the sunset,
And the birds, flocking together, return home.
Among all these things there is a very real meaning,

But, when I try to describe it,
I become lost in "no-words."*

This is a wonderful example of the true meditative state of mind functioning in the natural world around us. Such a condition is reached by regular practice of meditation, which has stilled the waves of the mind so that the affecting natural scene has imprinted itself thereon, without the mind in any way being influenced by intellection, conceptualization, or memory. In such a state it reflects things exactly as they are, the way a still pond reflects the flight of geese overhead — unintentionally and accurately.

Here the mind is one-pointed, focused on only one object to the exclusion of all others. This conditon can be reached by intense concentration on a Mantra (formula of sound), fixation on an internal or external point of the body (such as the diaphragm in the rising and falling of the breathing process), or thru unbroken concentration on a vexatious problem known as a Koan in Zen practice ("If all things return to the One, to where does that One return?" is a representative beginner's Koan). The focus of the mind on only one thought, in which the mind merges with its object (according to Indian concept), results in the one-pointed state in which the meditator is fully alive and aware, but reacts to only one stimulus. In Zen meditation, all other sights and sounds are appreciated, but there is no reactive tendency to them. And then, when the mind has become one-pointed and fully concentrated, the great miracle may take place and the mind becomes "no-pointed" (Mushin — no mind), blissfully lost in the state of no thought, far beyond the disturbing reactions of the senses.

*_Creativity and Taoism_ (Julian Press)
Translation: Chang Chung-Yuan

In Indian meditation it is a trance state; in Zen and Buddhist concentration, it is a condition of "choiceless awareness," which Krishnamurti has cited as the "true meditation." It is a state that cannot be described in language, hence the poet's statement: "I get lost in no-words."

Is it a "happy state?" Certainly not in the sense of pleasure and pain, which are only two sides of the same coin. But to determine if it affords a higher level of peace and equanimity, let's examine one more Chinese poem in a translation by the same scholar:

When the mind is transparent and pure,
As if reflected on the mirror-like surface of the water,
There is nothing in the world that you would dislike.
When it is serene as the light breeze in the sunshine,
There will be no-one whom you would like to forget.

Surely this is a state to be envied. The great teachers of meditation all tell us that, without exception, it can be ours if we create the right conditions and unfalteringly practice the type of meditation that is best for us.

We can approach this state thru the mind (as in Zen meditation or Mantra repetition) or thru the physical organism (as in T'ai Chi Chih, T'ai Chi Ch'uan, and the secret Nei Kung). Either way, the ultimate result is the same. The mind-body continuum is stilled and the inherent wisdom shines forth without hindrance.

Though the ultimate reward is the same, the immediate effects vary widely. In Indian meditation (such as Japa and the Breath-Dhyana), we reach a condition known as the Turiya state, the unchanging fourth state of consciousness that underlies the ordinary waking, dreaming, and deep sleep states. These latter three, which the average person experiences at different times, are not constant as they last for only short periods of time and are bewildering in the profusion of different, often painful, phenomena they produce. Carrying our "self" is a great load at all times in these three states, and we have the unutterable relief of laying down the ego burden in this type of meditation. The stresses of strain and tension, worry and fear are unraveled with corresponding relief to the physical organism. Carrying this painful ego burden and its many problems is somewhat like pouring water in a small jar and floating it in the sea. The water in the jar is separate from that of the sea around, bobbing up and down aimlessly on the surface of the water. But let us break the sides of the bottle, and the water merges with the great ocean, without a particle of separation. Similarly, the "individual consciousness" (if we can invent an almost meaningless phrase) in the state of deepest meditation, when the Turiya state is being experienced, becomes one with Universal Consciousness and is in its natural condition. Practiced daily, the type of meditation that takes us to this state (eyes closed, breath subsiding as the mind merges in one-pointedness with its object) is healing from the standpoint of relieving stress on the nervous system. It is not healing in the way that some of the Chinese meditations are (circulating and balancing the Chi). Such type of "trance meditation" should be followed by physical movement or posture that *does* cause the intrinsic energy to flow smoothly. If there is long practice of the trance state without the offsetting physical stimulus, illness may result.

As we see from the above, meditation is the focusing of the mind on one thought, to the exclusion of all others. It is usually practiced in absolute body stillness, but such is not the case with "moving meditations." When the Indian sage, Patanjali, talks about "inhibition or cessation of mental modifications," he is talking about the end of the reactive tendencies of the mind, whether in trance state (as in Japa) or in a reactionless state of heightened awareness (as in Zen). In either case he is saying that the mind is perfect and complete when no habit energies are being formed, when no new "grooves" are being formed from apperception, and when, as a result of the above, no long lasting (thru many lives, believe the Orientals) tendencies are developed. In order to understand what meditation is, and why it works, it is necessary to examine the meaning of such Sanskrit words as Vritti, Vashana, and Samskara. The meanings of these words will give us a clue as to what meditation really is and what happens with continued practice.

In India it is said that every thought results in a sound, which is imprinted on the brain (deeply or otherwise) as a Vritti, a groove, which explains the fact that we can recall experience afterward in memory. In the Bible, the phrase "In the Beginning was the Word" seemingly points to the same idea. Since both the Indian and the Chinese believe that first comes the thought, then the sound (and flow of Chi), followed by the manifestation (in the body, the flow of blood), we have a concept that points both at creation (the first manifestation of being) and the physical functioning of the individual. In Indian cosmology, it is believed that all this (the cosmos) is the "thought of Brahma," that is, from the initial thought came the sound that resulted in the flow of Prana (Chi) which has shaped this and other universes.

As the mind becomes one pointed in meditation, the Vritti becomes widened and intensified and becomes habit energy (Vashana), which not only governs our everyday life, but actually ' shapes our bodies and personalities and makes us what we are. An analogy to this is the following: If we continually take a short-cut thru a field of deep, waving grass, gradually a path will be made, and it will be easy for us to get thru it. The first walk across the field was equivalent to the Vritti and the following walks, widening the path, corresponded to the habit energy, the Vashana. Eventually we become used to following the "easy way," the path or shortcut, and our habit of going that way becomes deeply imbedded. Others may follow this path, even after our death; it may become a road. This is the Samskara, the tendency that goes on life after life unless stern practice of meditation annuls it (unless we stop using the shortcut thru the fields and allow the long grass to grow together again).

Translated into human terms, we have this example: A man, experiencing great disappointment, turns to drink and finds the clouding effects of the alcohol help him to forget his troubles. He gets used to reacting to any disappointment by taking a few drinks, thus building the Vashana (habit energy) of drinking. Carried to an extreme, where he becomes an unknowing alcoholic, he has created the Samskara (tendency) that may follow him and influence him thru "future lives," causing him to become an unwilling drunkard without even knowing why he drinks. Only stern discipline, over a good period of time, can erase such tendency for, if he simply takes himself away from the environment in which he drinks, or removes himself from the proximity of alcohol, this may dim the Vashana, but the Samskara will still remain and become active when the proper circumstances manifest again. Thus we have the monk in the desert (as in Anatole France's *Thais*) who has completely removed himself from carnal thoughts (Vashanas), but has not erased the tendencies so that, when the mind is ready, once again the sensuous temptations enter his thought, even after he was certain he had done away with them. Removing one's self from temptation will, necessarily, stunt the habit energy, but, as long as the tendency is not done away with (the "seeds of Karma" are not burned), there is always the probability that the habit will reestablish itself in the future.

Two things now become apparent to us. Thru concentration and affirmation we can shape our thoughts to bring about whatever we want in the future, providing they are strong enough to counter the existing habit energies and tendencies. We can plant any seed we want, knowing that, in time, we will harvest the fruit. This does not take enthusiasm; it demands steadfastness and continual practice, not only in periods of meditation, but in all times when the mind is active.

Also, thru care in how the mind thinks and thru frequent and regular meditation, we can undo the negative traits that have been established in the mind — that is, we can nullify the Vashanas and eventually eliminate the undesirable Samskaras. This is the "raison d'etre" of meditation, and this is what is meant by Patanjali when he talks of the "inhibition or cessation of mental modifications." These "mental modifications" are the Vrittis which become Vashanas, eventually resulting in the long-lasting tendencies known as Samskaras. For the monk, who may work toward total abstraction, the idea is to erase these modifications, to eliminate the Karma that is keeping him bound, thus reaching total liberation.

Most of us, however, are not monks and renunciates, so we wish to be able to shape the habit energies so as to have more fulfilling lives. Therefore, we are careful at all times, and we meditate. In meditation, we concentrate on one object to the exclusion of all others. Thus we build one big Vashana that overpowers all the others; we become one-pointed in that which is pleasing to us and points the way to our becoming what we wish to be. In such a way we reshape our world. The mind making all things, we let it dwell on the chosen object and it becomes that which we have decided upon as our ideal. As we say, this demands persistance and steadfastness. So we work and live in the world in control of what we become — and thus are masters of our Karma, not pulled willy-nilly by tendencies that are beyond the conscious understanding. This really is the deepest, and most practical, form of psychology (as many doctors and psychologists are learning). It is the way to heal ourselves and remake ourselves thru meditation. One-pointed concentration, and its aftermath, afford the answer.

Chapter 3
CLASSIFICATION — DIFFERENT MODES OF MEDITATION

Few people, and particularly teachers, have had the opportunity to be exposed to diverse types of meditation, so that many do not know that there *are* different forms. Far fewer have had the opportunity to experience — and train in — more than one type, so that whatever they know has been necessarily biased in favor of the one activity they have experienced. The Indian Saddhaka (aspirant) believed all Dhyana (meditation) is intense concentration on an aspect of God, though such does not at all enter most Chinese varieties of meditation. The Chinese are greatly concerned with circulation and control of the Chi, while Japanese Zen, though derived from the Chinese Ch'anna seems to have lost sight of this particular aspect of practice. There is one type of meditation practiced by Tibetan monks that has as its sole aim the ability to consciously leave the body thru an opening at the top of the head (sometimes know as the "aperture of Brahma") at the time of death. Needless to say, we are not concerned with such esoteric practice in this book; our purpose is to instruct the reader in techniques of meditation that are comparatively simple to practice, and that will most probably result in better health, physically and psychically.

Suffice to say, there are innumerable types of

meditation, including some that might better be called concentration or silent chanting. For the purposes of this book we have arbitrarily divided the meditations we are to consider into nine types, as follows:

1. CIRCULATING THE CHI FOR HEALING The Nei Kung usually is practiced while lying flat on the back with eyes closed and legs pressed together. It can be done in cross-legged meditative pose, but the best time to practice Nei Kung is in bed at night before going to sleep. The name literally means "inner efficiency," and the reason for this title will be easily discerned when one has practiced it a few times. Generally, the practicer will fall asleep while repeating the mental affirmations. He may awaken during the night with a strong heat flowing thru him, and that heat has great healing qualities. Wherever the heat is felt, there is said to be blockage. As the Chi energy flows thru the body from just below the waist down to the soles of the feet (the so-called "bubbling spring"), it passes thru the meridian channels which are the basis of Chinese acupuncture. Effects are strong, and surprising to the beginner.

2. WORKING WITH THE BREATH The Great Circle Meditation, along with another form of meditative breathing, together make up what we call Reverse Meditative Breathing. We recommend that this type of breathing be practiced as a preliminary to all other meditations, for it stills the mind and makes it easily pliable. There is also a form in the moving meditation, T'ai Chi Chih, known as The Joyous Breath, and this can be practiced, while standing, as a preliminary to other forms. The Reverse Meditative Breathing, while an excellent preliminary, is itself a meditation of the highest efficacy and can lead to a state of deep immersion. It is energizing and generally should not be done just before bedtime, as it

may prevent restful sleep. The healing effects will be obvious to the one practicing it regularly. There are deep spiritual effects, too, as the first part of the Reverse Meditative Breathing is almost synonymous with the developing of the Golden Flower, the immortal spirit body spoken of in such esoteric works as *The Secret of the Golden Flower* — only the movement of the eyes is different. In particular, these meditative breathing practices make an excellent preliminary to Mantra meditation (Japa). Those who do not now obtain good results regularly with the latter should find that these breathings greatly increase the efficiency of their own form of meditation.

3. MANTRA AND BREATH COUNTING The many types of Mantra repetition have, as their highest practice, the mental repetition of the divine name. Practiced regularly, this will take one into a state of thoughtless pure consciousness, a latent awareness with no subject-object relationship at work. Strangely enough, the Breath Dhyana (a technique of counting either inbreaths or outbreaths) will achieve the same result. For those who shy away from such things as the "Divine Name," this is a way of achieving pure consciousness (the so-called fourth state of consciousness) without resorting to any holy or theistically-inclined practice.

Such practices as the Nembutsu of Japanese Shinshu Buddhism, and the repetition of a phrase from the Lotus Sutra (scripture) in Nichiren Buddhism of Japan (now spreading thru the Western world), can be said to be Mantra meditations, as well. In Christianity, the "Hail Mary" can have the same effect. In all cultures we find practices based on repetition of holy names.

4. MINDFULNESS This principally has to do with the Buddha's great meditation, the Satipatthana, and

derivatives of it, such as the short Vipassyana practice and the so-called Burmese Method. Here we enter the deepest realms of psychology. The Satipatthana, in effect, is practiced in every waking moment, and it increases the awareness of one's body and responses to a tremendous degree, with the natural concommitant of improved health and state of mind. To *know* what is actually happening, rather than unconsciously floating thru daily activities, bears out the saying "The Truth shall set you free." Zen (Ch'an in Chinese) is probably an outgrowth of the Way of Mindfulness, but it developed its own characteristics in China in the T'ang Dynasty (roughly 600-900 A.D.).

5. FIXATION Intense Concentration and forming of a "view" take place in the Chih-K'uan meditation of Chinese T'ien T'ai Buddhism. This seemingly simple concentrative practice is much more profound than is apparent. It greatly increases our awareness and, regularly practiced, often results in flashes of insight into the nature of reality. Very healing in a bodily (and psychological) sense, it is the outcome of a complicated healing system developed by T'ien T'ai Buddhists.

There is a meditation that the author has developed that utilizes the Yin (negative force) of the earth and the Yang (positive force) of the sun and sky. It utilizes intense concentration on the "third eye" spot and visualization of the two forces entering thru top of the head and soles of the feet. It is called the "Earth-Sky" meditation.

6. VISUALIZATION The author elaborates on the mental visualization he used to develop the Dumo Heat of Tibetan Tantric Buddhism, a practice that lasted a year and one-half. This inner heat — which is developed in somewhat less concentrated manner in moving meditations such as T'ai Chi Chih — is tremendously healing. While the author does not suggest that the beginner practice the

whole discipline, there may be suggestions which will prove useful in his healing practice.

7. CHANTING Single-minded oral repetition of such phrases as the Gayatri, the Japanese Nembutsu, the passage from the Lotus Sutra, the Heart Sutra of Buddhism, and other well-known works, can be strongly effective in relieving tensions and bringing the mind to a one-pointed state. Moreover, various affirmations are effective when repeated mentally on a regular basis; they strongly affect the subconscious mind. One Indian sage has said that such repetitions while the breath is held have the greatest strength and are very efficacious, particularly where a name of God is concerned.

8. MIND CONTROL Zen is the meditation sect of Buddhism, and all Zen practice has to do with mind control. We will speak briefly of the effects of the puzzling Koan practice, but will not suggest that a Zen aspirant practice it without the guidance of a Zen master. However, the four-part meditation of Zen Master Rinzai (his Chinese name was Lin Chi) is subtle and can be very helpful in stabilizing the state of mind. It also tends to lead to insights of considerable value, and well illustrates the "neither nor" attitude of Buddhist meditative practice.

9. MOVING MEDITATION T'ai Chi Chih and T'ai Chi Ch'uan are moving meditations of great beauty and have profound effects upon the physical organism. There seems to be no better way to nullify the effects of aging, to stay healthy, and to have a joyous frame of mind at most times. It is easy for the practicer to realize the numerous physical benefits of these forms — in weight control, cultivation of energy, development of serenity — but he is usually not aware of the great psychological and spiritual effects that effortlessly take place. Probably there are no more beneficial and practical meditative practices for West-

erners, as these do not demand silence or enforced inaction of the practicer. Moving easily and joyously, he derives all the effects of meditation, and the forms can be done anywhere at any time. T'ai Chi Chih, particularly, needs no special conditions; all one has to do is stand up and move while remaining in one place. There are many of the benefits of Hatha Yoga and Kundalini Yoga in these practices, without any of the difficulties and drawbacks. No special mental preparation or frame of mind is required. The concentration of mind, while moving, on the Tan T'ien (just below the navel), or in the soles of the feet, brings strong physical effects.

As stated, these are arbitrary classifications, but they should be effective to help the reader know about different types of meditation and to be able to choose that most compatible with his goals. It should be helpful to doctors, psychologists, educators, and spiritual leaders who are engaged in holistic activities, leading to better health of the mind and psyche. It is to be hoped that it leads to the understanding that there is not one but many, many modes of meditation, and other practices that develop into meditation. It is felt the different classifications will help the reader, and the prospective meditator, to establish priorities and spend his time on those types of meditation which promise the rewards he wishes. It must be remembered that all are valid and all are viable, and all meditation has some healing qualities.

The question now arises: "Why are there so many different types of meditation?"

The answer is twofold. First, there are different objectives in meditating; hence the need for different forms of meditation. The greater reason, however, has to do with the vast difference in the traditions, temperaments, climates, and general environment of those who "originated" these meditations.

The temperament of most of the people of India lends itself to devotional practices. The very nature of life in India leads in this direction. From the strict caste system to the many forms of religion practiced under the generic name Hindu (which includes Sikhs, Tantriks, Jains, worshipers of god Shiva and of god Vishnu, and more), everything in India clothes the everyday way of life with awe and propitiation of deities. Even the Vedanta, which in the beginning was extremely intellectual in espousing only the nonduality known as Advaita (a formless way that is far beyond the average man's comprehension), gradually widened to include such deviations as the worship of Divine Mother practiced by Ramakrishna followers. The Indian wants something concrete in his spiritual practices, and so he has a multitude of gods, all supposedly representing aspects of the One Reality, from which he can choose and to which he can sublimate himself. The great world religion, Buddhism, is an atheistic religion, though, in time, after the death of Gautama the Buddha, a devotion to Buddha and to the Buddha of Infinite Light and Life (nonhistoric) did develop. Essentially, Buddhism is nondualistic and nondevotional, however, and, primarily for this reason, the great world religion has all but disappeared from the subcontinent of India. It has found good homes in other parts of the world where the abstract is more understood and where personal devotion does not mean as much, but the character of the Indian does not accord with the way of the Buddha. It is dry and without emotion to him, whereas the way of devotion (Bhakti) stirs the heart and kindles the emotion (and many delusions with it). It is natural that most meditations developed by Indians rely either on remembrance of a name of God

(Mantra) or concentration on the supposed aspects of the various deities. Both of these paths fit into traditional Dhyana (meditation) and are ultimately based on devotion. Not all Westerners wish to develop such devotion, however, particularly to foreign-sounding deities. For them, Mantra meditation is not the best way, though some of those who are "selling" such meditative Japa mistakenly insist it has nothing to do with religion and has no connection with Yoga. Actually, meditation with a Mantra is the height of Yoga (Yoga Shastra) and repetition of the name of God can hardly be said to have no religious implications.

The Chinese people are very practical in nature. In the beginning of spiritual contacts with India, they were amazed by the high-flying imagery and great metaphysical imagination of the Indian people. The concept of an overall God who was the manifested aspect of the formless Brahman (reality) was not possible for the Chinese. He was sensitive to nature and the natural world, and did not share the renunciate tendencies of his western neighbor. Cultured equally by the pragmatic social teachings of Confucius and the mysticism of Taoism, the Chinese could picture a Way, but it was not the Way of a personal God. The meditations that grew from Taoism and Buddhism — such as the Zazen of the Ch'an (Zen) school, the one-pointed fixation of T'ien T'ai, and the circulation and mixing of the vital force (Chi) in the Taoist form of Alchemy — were far different from those practiced by the Indians. Many Chinese, and later Japanese, sat long periods of meditation simply for the physical effects involved. Those who had been sick found they tended to recover from their illnesses when meditating regularly, and artisans and craftsmen found that simple meditative sitting, without any overtones of spirituality, tended to sharpen the intuition and creativity. The Samurai swordsman and the ritual swordmaker of Japan wanted something that would provide inspiration and take away the fear of death. These they found in plain sitting, and also in Zen meditation, which brought a fearlessness to those who might die at any time.

The Tibetan character has always been greatly influenced by magic, and many remnants of the old practices have remained in the cold country, so Tibetan meditation, using much imagination, visualization, and imagery, is far different from the Buddhist meditations of the warmer climes. It is interesting that the Tibetan practices eventually descended all the way to Japan, where the abstract Shingon Buddhist form of meditating on a circle with a written character growing out of a Lotus, along with elaborate ritual and formalism, captivated royalty and the nobles. However, the plainer people did not respond to such high-flown procedures (and probably never had the chance). For centuries, and today, the plainer people tend to follow a Way of Devotion, the remembrance of the name of Amida (the Buddha of Infinite Light) in the hope that His vow to save all beings will take them to the Pure Land, the Western Paradise when they die. The Nembutsu, constant repetition of the phrase "Namu Amida Butsu," is a tremendously effective meditation, starting as a Mantra repetition and eventually culturing the heart to where the phrase goes on day and night inside the real devotee.

So it may be said that many temperaments in the Orient have contributed to the techiniques of meditation. No two peoples could be farther apart than the Indians and the Japanese; yet the Buddhism of India, which died in its native land, later found a home in the Japanese Islands, where it has been the single greatest force in creating Japanese culture.

The religious examples above are not important to the reader who wishes to use the techniques for his own benefit without participating in any of the beliefs which led to their development. Nevertheless, most meditation has been derived from spiritual activities; it is hard to separate them. The Westerner will usually be more interested in the practical doing than in acquiring knowledge of the origin and real meanings of the practices, but such knowledge can be helpful, and in many cases will motivate the meditator. Usually, he should derive great physical benefits from meditation; he may also gain other rewards that he had not counted on, and the effects of these may be stronger than he imagines. Together they can help to make him whole and change him from a suffering being to a joyful one.

Chapter 4
CIRCULATING THE CHI
Instruction and Commentary

The "secret" Nei Kung (pronounced "nei gung" in Chinese and "nai kan" in Japanese) is a comparatively simple meditation that has great healing properties. It is little known because it is generally considered part of an oral tradition; that is, it is usually taught by teacher directly to disciple and not written about. Nei Kung literally means "inner efficiency," and it has almost disappeared in Japan, though one of the greatest Japanese Zen masters, Hakuin Zenji, wrote about it very explicitly and used it to great advantage in the 18th Century.

Hakuin attributed his recovery from illness, when he was a young man, to the instruction in the Nei Kung given him by a fascinating teacher who lived in a cave in the mountains near Shirakawa (White River Junction) in one of the coldest parts of Japan. This mountain hermit (known as "Sennin" in Japan) was said to be over two hundred years old, and would often go without food for considerable lengths of time, as indeed he was doing when Hakuin arrived at his mountain cave after a long and difficult journey.

The Sennin taught Hakuin how to circulate and balance the Chi, vital force, and how to bring the "heart-fire" down (the heart being the great Yang, or positive force, corresponding to the heat of the sun) rather than letting the Yin (negative force) of the kidney region rise. This is pure Chinese Taoism, and the origin of acupuncture, but Zen admittedly owes much to Taoism.

Not only did this practice enable Zen Master Hakuin to regain his health, which had broken down due to too much intensive concentration on "Truth" (according to the mountain master), but it also enabled him to make his breakthru in Zen practice, years later, leading to the many Satori (sudden enlightenment) experiences he was to enjoy. Under the circumstances, since Hakuin revitalized all Japanese Zen in modern times, it seems strange that the Nei Kung has practically disappeared in Japan. The author found none — layman, monk, or master — who practice it in the present day.

The Nei Kung can be performed sitting in cross-legged meditative pose (as the Sennin, the mountain master, was doing, seemingly making him impervious to hunger and to the extreme cold of the mountain winter) but, for healing purposes, the best way is to do it at night, in bed, before going to sleep. The practice will put you to sleep! If it could be bottled, it would make a great substitute for sleeping pills.

Often one who practices the Nei Kung, after falling asleep, will awaken in the middle of the night with a strange heat surging thru him. This heat is very healing. At other times, when walking or sitting quietly, one may feel the heat at the base of the skull, as a flush in the cheeks, or in the various limbs. Wherever it is strongly felt, there is usually "blockage." The energy is flowing freely thru the meridian channels, then comes to a blockage or injury and manifests as a healing heat. This is the Chi at work. This is much the same as the energy of electricity that flows until it is blocked, then becomes the electric light.

This bodily heat is not only healing, it is energizing as well. One may wake the next morning, after practice, with great amounts of energy.

To practice Nei Kung we simply have to memorize the four affirmations below, not a very difficult task, If terms such as "Pure Land" or "Amida Buddha" are upsetting, it is possible to substitute any names that appeal to the reader. Otherwise, it is best to do the practice as given, without any thought of the results — then be surprised by the effects that develop. The Buddha is supposed to have said "He who can keep his concentration in the soles of his feet will heal 1000 illnesses." The meaning of this will become clear in practice, as the energy builds up and surges from below the navel to the soles of the feet (the "bubbling spring"). The spot below the navel is known as "Tan T'ien" in Chinese and "Tanden" in Japanese; we will use the Japanese word because it seems easier.

INSTRUCTION

Lying on your back, in bed, with eyes closed and the room light turned off, press your legs together and begin to mentally repeat the following four affirmations, over and over, until sleep intervenes:

1. This Energy Sea, this Tanden, from below the navel to the soles of the feet, full of my Original Face; where are the nostrils on that face?

2. This Energy Sea, this Tanden, from below the navel to the soles of the feet, full of my True Home; what need of a message from that home?

3. This Energy Sea, this Tanden, from below the navel to the soles of the feet, full of the Pure Land of Consciousness only; what need of outer pomp for this Pure Land?

Infinite Compassion

4. This Energy Sea, this Tanden, from below the navel to the soles of the feet, full of the Amida Buddha of heart and body; what sermon would this Amida be preaching?

COMMENTARY

When these formulae are repeated over and over, the effect should take place automatically; any deliberate effort to make it happen, however, will prevent it from doing so. That effect, in the author's opinion, is as healing as any practice that can be performed. All that is needed is regularity. The practicer will note that, as time goes by, he becomes oblivious to the cold around him and develops an inner heat that somewhat corresponds to the Dumo Heat of Tibet. If only medical doctors would have their patients use the healing potential of the Nei Kung!

A few words of explanation about the terms used above seems in order: "Energy Sea" refers to the area just below the navel, where the Chi energy is stored. It is the seat of intuition, and the Chinese credit it with greatly influencing creativity. Healing practice is usually based on the flow of the Chi and this will flow from the Energy Sea or Tanden (same place) down to the "Bubbling Spring" at the soles of the feet. It is interesting that the Tantriks of India worship this energy as the Shakti, having personalized this energy as the goddess who is the active, female side of the unchanging Reality, Shiva. There is no more useful practice than developing the ability to actively circulate this life force, whether it is by the Nei Kung thru mental practice, or by T'ai Chi Chih and T'ai Chi Ch'uan thru physical movement.

"Original Face" is a term that occurs in Zen Buddhism, particularly where there is practice with the Koan (a "case," or insoluble problem used in Rinzai Zen). "Show me your 'Original Face' before you were born!" is a famous admonition that Zen teachers have used, and it has become a favorite beginner's Koan in Zen practice, both in China and Japan. Of course, it means your True Self or "Buddha Nature."

The "Pure Land" refers to the Western Paradise in the Chinese Amitabha sect of Buddhism (known as "Shinshu" in Japan). Amitabha, whose name is "Amida" in Japanese, is the nonhistoric Buddha of Infinite Light. Gautama Buddha, the historic Buddha from India (who lived 2500 years ago), is supposed to have told his followers that, aeons ago, before recorded history, there was a great Bodhisattva (enlightened being, one on his way to becoming a Buddha) who took a vow that, if he should succeed in becoming a Buddha, he would save all beings and, if they remembered his name just ten times, he would take them, no matter how sinful they were, to the Western Paradise, the "Pure Land," when they died. There they would enjoy ideal conditions to continue their practice of Buddhism and eventually attain Nirvana.

Recently in Taiwan a master of about ninety died. Some years ago the author spent an interesting time with him, and believed him to be the last master of T'ai Chi Gik, a self-defense form of T'ai Chi in which he could paralyze an opponent by touching him in a particular spot, relative to the time of day and the season of the year. This would stop the flow of the vital force and leave the opponent helpless; if he struggled too much, he could endanger his own life, and it is believed that, for this reason, the practice was abolished.

This master, whose name was Liu, suggested lying nude on the earth, facing up to the sun, so as to take in the Yang (positive) of the sun and absorb the Yin (negative) of the earth at the same time. This is an excellent way to practice Nei Kung, for those who have the privacy to do so. The author treasures the writings, in Chinese, he received from Master Liu.

ANCIENT CHINESE SAGE-HEALER
From a painting by Hsu Wen-chang (1521-1593)
Ming dynasty painter and writer

Chapter 5
WORKING WITH THE BREATH
Instruction and Commentary

The two forms of Reverse Meditative Breathing play a dual role in "healing meditation." First, it is extremely useful as a preliminary to other types of meditation. If those who do Mantra meditation, for example, will perform the two Reverse Meditative Breaths before starting to use their Mantra, they will experience much greater success with their own meditation. In this busy world, a typical example is the following:

Arriving home in late afternoon, fresh off the crowded freeway, the meditator finds he has about 45 minutes before he has to dress for dinner, and decides to use this time for his customary afternoon sitting. His mind is full of the activities of the day, and his face shows the tension of driving thru heavy traffic — yet he immediately sits down, closes his eyes, and begins to repeat his Mantra, or practice whatever form of meditation he is doing. The mind does not turn off that easily, and soon memories of the day, plans for the morrow, and idle daydreaming intervene. If he is tired, the sudden relaxation may put him to sleep. In most cases, it will be difficult for the mind to be clear and still, not active but aware, so that he can meditate properly. It is difficult to have good meditations when the mind is fuzzy and dull, and this is particularly true of Mantra meditation.

In these circumstances, if he (or she) will do Reverse Meditative Breathing for five or ten minutes, he will be invigorated and the mind will probably cease its endless chatter; then, if he drops the Mantra into the ensuing silence, he should attain quick and effortless results. The effortless part is important, as effort in meditation has the opposite effect from that intended. It is the "effort of no-effort" that get results.

Many times the author, in his Comparative Meditation classes, has been amazed at how quickly newcomers attain the state of pure consciousness when working with a Mantra for the first time — if they preceded their meditation with practice of the two Reverse Meditative Breaths. This is true whether their basic meditation is harmonizing a Mantra with the breath, doing Manasika Japa (TM), or using the Breath-Dhyana. Often in just eight minutes of silent practice, three-quarters of the beginning meditators have "entered" this Pure State of Consciousness (called "transcending" in TM). This is a remarkable result. Many Yogis the author has met in India feel it takes 10 to 20 years to attain this state. It is all possible because the mind has been stilled by a few minutes practice of the Reverse Meditative Breathing as a preliminary to the practicer's own basic meditation.

These two circulating breaths have great power on their own. Finishing the nine orbits, one is usually in a state of great quietude, so it is obvious that the breaths comprise a meditation of real power. In some ways they approximate the "backward flowing method" of the Tibetans and Chinese, transmuting the sex energy into something higher. For this reason, the Reverse Meditative Breathing is greatly energizing and will interfere with sound sleep, therefore should not be performed just before bedtime. There is one exception to the rule: One time when the author was staying at a Ramakrishna Ashram, he came across a young Yogi who was greatly troubled by the frequent emissions he was having at night. Having taken a vow of celibacy and continence, these sexual emissions caused a real feeling of guilt in him; still, it is hard for a healthy 22 year old not to have this outlet. The problem was solved when the author taught him "The Great Circle Meditation" (first part of the Reverse Meditative Breaths) and suggested that he deliberately wake himself each night at 1 a.m. and do this Macrocosmic Orbit nine times. From that day forward the nightly ejaculations stopped, and the young Yogi remarked on the tremendous energy with which he awoke each morning. This was a graphic example of using these breaths to transmute the sexual energy (and the psychic activity that goes with it) into something more suitable for a spiritual renunciate.

For most people, obviously, this is not necessary. Few of us are practicing Yogis. In later chapters, when we learn the Moving Meditations (particularly T'ai Chi Chih), we will find that the vital force is definitely stimulating sexually, capable of turning impotence into a very real potency. In such case, the Reverse Meditative Breaths should not be practiced more than once a day (early morning is best) or just before regular meditation. The male or female who *wants* this increased sexual energy will probably not wish to sublimate or transmute it.

From the Chinese viewpoint, importance of the Reverse Meditative Breath can be surmised when we know that the ultimate in meditation is to mix the Essence, Vitality, and Spirit (Ching Chi Shen) so as to attain to immortality. This is exactly what we are doing in the orbits of the two Reverse Meditative Breaths.

With these thoughts, let us proceed to the instruction in the Reverse Meditative Breathing.

INSTRUCTION (Part One)

We are going to begin with a visualization so that the meditator will get the feel of the "warm golden light" we will work with. It is what the Chinese teachers call "The True Thought," and is immensely self-healing.

First, close your eyes. Now imagine that you, the meditator, are seated on a fleecy white cloud, which comes up over your hips. It is soft and buoyant, and gradually it lifts you off the ground as it begins to soar aloft.

Up and up goes the cloud, with you seated comfortably on it. Now, high above, you see a great waterfall in the sky, a waterfall of warm golden light cascading down. Gradually your cloud approaches the base of the waterfall, and now, as you reach it, the moist warm golden light pours down over your head. You are engulfed by the golden light.

The warm feeling breaks down thru the top of your skull, down past the eyes, the nose, the mouth, and the chin. Bathing you internally with warm golden light, it goes down past the shoulders, the chest, and the abdomen, coming to rest in the Tan T'ien two inches below the navel.

After resting there a minute, the warm golden light rises to the belt and splits in two, one part going to the right and one to the left.

Reaching the sides, the two rays start down again, past the two hips, to the thighs, the knees, the calves, and the ankles, finally reaching the soles of the feet. And there you sit, with the soles of the feet bathed in warm golden light. All this should be vividly visualized.

After a moment's pause, we bring the light up the inside of the leg, passing the ankles, the calves, the knees, and the thighs — then reaching the crotch and coming together in the Tan T'ien below the navel.

Now the light goes between the legs to the base of the spine, and begins a slow ascent, thrilling each cell of the back as it works its way up toward the head. From the base of the spine the moist-warm thought proceeds to the small of the back, the middle of the back, the shoulder blades, the shoulders, and the base of the skull (where there is often great blockage). From the neck where the skull begins, it rises slowly until it reaches the top of the head, where it rests, splashing down like a golden shower over and thru the head. We have now returned to where we began, having made a "grand orbit." This is the best way for the meditator to start each day, having the waterfall crash down over the skull, and then the warm golden light work its way down to the soles of the feet, then back up to the top of the head. This should be performed once, and then the smaller Macrocosmic Orbit should be followed. Generally we perform these circles nine times (nine is the positive number for the Chinese), but even three times can be effective.

At this point the meditator must decide if he has the feel of the warm golden light, or if he wants his cloud to make another ascent into the base of the waterfall so that the visualization may become more vivid.

If the "proper thought" can now be easily experienced, we should begin the smaller Macrocosmic Orbit, which will make up the bulk of our practice. The trip to the soles of the feet is valuable, and some practicers begin by "breathing" in thru the soles of the feet (or even the sexual organ) and beginning the ascent from there. However, the smaller orbit (our main practice) will start in the Tan T'ien. After our first trip, utilizing the waterfall and the descent to the feet, we will be content with a circle that goes from the small of the back to the top of the head, and then down the front to the spot below the navel.

We begin this smaller orbit by starting at the Tan T'ien, taking the light between the legs, and then slowly up the back. Rest at the top of the head for a moment or two, then come back down the front to the spot two inches below the navel. Continue this orbit eight more times, adding the proper action of the breath, the eyes, and the anus, as descibed below.

The Breath. As the light starts up the back, touching every cell, we begin to breathe in, expanding the chest and the abdomen as we do so. By the time the light reaches the top of the head (where we rest), we have breathed in as much as possible and expanded greatly. At the top of the head we hold the breath. This is an excellent time to insert a mental affirmation or formula, if desired. Then start down by exhaling thru the nose, with the mouth closed, in four sections. That is, as we breathe out a little, the light comes down to the chin; then we breathe out some more and the light reaches the chest; breathe out some more (contracting as we do so) and the light reaches the diaphragm; and, finally, as all the breath is expelled, the light reaches the Tan T'ien. We rest there with the stomach contracted tightly against the backbone.

As we come down in four sections, the breath will be easily heard as it is audibly expelled thru the nose. We come down in levels because if we let out all the breath at once as the light descends, there would immediately be a reflex in-breath. This way the breath is out, the stomach and the chest contracted, and we feel as though we could rest all day in the great emptiness at the Tan T'ien.

Eyes. Now that we have mastered the expanding-inhaling breath going up and the contracting-exhaling breath coming down in four levels, we can learn the correct eye movements. These movements of the eyes take place *even though the eyes are closed.*

As we take the light up the spine, and breathe in, we raise the eyes, using them as a lever to bring the light up.

We begin with the eyes (which are closed) focused on the Tan T'ien below. Then, as the light comes up the back and we breathe in, the eyes are gradually raised until they are turned to the top of the head as the light reaches the top and the breath is full and held. In effect, we feel as though the action of the eyes is bringing the light up the back.

Starting down the front, as we breathe out in four levels, the eyes gradually are lowered, until, by the time the light is back in the Tan T'ien, the eyes are once more focused in that direction.

The Anus. There is one more action to learn in making this smaller orbit. When the light, having come thru the legs to the backbone, starts slowly up the spine (and we breathe in and raise our eyes), we contract muscles of the anus and hold them tight until the light reaches the top of the head. Then, after the pause, as the light starts down (with the breath being exhaled in four sections and the eyes being lowered), we relax the muscles of the anus gradually, until they are again normal as the light again reaches the Tan T'ien.

All this takes time to learn, but it is not really complicated. We begin by visualizing the waterfall and taking the light to the feet, then back up the spine to the head, but with each circle thereafter, we start from the Tan T'ien, take the light thru the legs, and start up the back, taking proper action with the breath, the eyes, and the anus. We then come back down to the spot below the navel where we began, being careful to come down in four sections.

This is a powerful meditation by itself. Nine orbits will usually leave one in a serene, restful state. As explained above, it does have the power of rousing the Kundalini, thus causing sexual excitement. However, it balances that by the fact that it transmutes this sexual excitement into a higher form of energy.

INSTRUCTION (Part Two)

Now we are going to learn the second part of the Reverse Meditative Breaths. This is much simpler, but we first will have to discuss the meaning behind the movements.

It is believed in India that there are two channels ("Nadis" in Indian terminology) that reach from the left and right eye down to the spot between the legs, below the sex organ. They are called "ida" and "pingala," and they are said to crisscross in figure eights on the way down to the terminus between the legs. However, for our purposes we will visualize them as being straight.

The instrinsic energy known as Prana or Chi is said to descend and ascend thru these channels in the average person, roughly corresponding with the breaths. However, in the case of an enlightened saint or sage, the Prana is said to at times come up thru a hair-thin central channel known as the Sushumna. Such saint-poets as the Tibetan Milarepa have written of the great ecstasy that is felt when the vital force rises thru the central channel. This is supposed to be much greater than the ecstasy of sexual climax, and, for the enlightened one, it frequently lasts for long periods of time (in the Tibetan practice known as the Left-Hand Tantra, utilizing a "backward flowing method," this bliss is deliberately cultivated thru an unusual sexual contact without discharge).

It is necessary for us to know this, because we are going to take the breath down thru the outside channels and then "shoot it" up the center, visualizing it entering the Sushumna, or central channel.

We begin by imagining the warm golden light starting

on our right side and our left side, at the heart level, and working down the outside channels, as we breathe in and expand. The light is visualized as going down, though the breath is being taken in. When the light reaches the spot below the sex organ (and the two sides merge there), we rest a moment, and then contracting the anus tightly, we shoot the light up the middle channel as we breathe out and contract the stomach and chest. Going down the sides (really, two lights) we breathe in and expand; shooting up the center, we breathe out in *four sections* (as we did in the previous breath) and raise the light to the heart level (not beyond) as we contract. There is no eye motion with this Breath, but the eyes are closed so that we may vividly visualize what we are doing.

This is an immensely powerful breath, and it is suggested that it not be performed more than nine times. It does stimulate sexual energy (which the other breath can transmute, if so desired), and may even cause psychic experiences at first. However, we have no interest in these and ignore them.

The two breaths together are greatly revitalizing, and should heighten the energy level considerably. Moreover, they are calming to the meditator, who may enter a period of abstraction (meditation) after doing them. Nine times doing each breath, followed by a period of serene rest in the emptiness one usually feels, is not only revitalizing, but tends to stimulate creativity and intuition.

It is suggested that the meditator start all meditation sessions with these breaths, or with the chanting of something like the Gayatri (Chapter 10) followed by these breaths, and then perform his own form of meditation. Remember, it is best not to do these breaths before going to sleep at night.

COMMENTARY

The reader should not worry about any of the references made to visions, sexual stimulus, or arousing of the Kundalini. These were made with the idea of educating the reader as to all possibilities, but with most meditators, doing the Reverse Meditative Breathing will be a happy and profound experience. Thought and breath are two sides of the same coin; when the breath is stilled, the mind is usually stilled. Often the mind is stilled to such an extent that, if the meditator wishes to follow the breaths with the Breath-Dhyana or a Mantra harmonized with the breath, he may find difficulty in detecting the natural breath. This is a good sign; immersion in meditation usually occurs when the breath has become almost nonexistent. In Samadhi, the "super-conscious state," there is no visible breathing at all, and this state is usually associated with great bliss, apperceived by the meditator after coming out of Samadhi.

Whether the two breaths be treated as ends in themselves, or used as preliminaries to other meditations, they have great validity and can contribute to a state of equanimity that is very salutary for the health.

Chapter 6
MANTRA AND BREATH COUNTING
Instruction and Commentary

A Mantra is a special formula, a word or group of words possessed of great power. It represents a name or aspect of God, and was supposedly revealed to a sage in India after long periods of austerity and meditative discipline. Most high-caste Indians have been initiated into their Mantras by their family teachers; some use them for meditation, some for constant repetition to encourage devotion, and others for near-magical powers.

Buddhists, who do not believe in an overall God, also have their Mantras, which they call "Dharani." The "Om Mani Padme Hum" of Tibet, the "Gate Gate Paragate Parasamgate Bodhi Svaha" of India, and the "Namu Amida Butsu" and "Namu Myo Ho Renge Kyo" of Japan do not have the theistic background of Hindu Mantras, but the purpose is the same. Remembrance of God, or remembrance of great teacher Buddha, both cultivate faith and devotion in the hearts of adherents.

In India, a Mantra is generally conferred by a teacher thru initiation, at a ceremony known as "Puja"; the Mantra the disciple receives is the one he uses for the rest of his life. In Buddhism such is not the case. When a Zen aspirant is given a Koan (problem) to solve, it is generally by a teacher and he confers with that teacher on the solution, but he is free to work with his own choice of Koan, if he wants, and, in the same way, he can use any Dharani (Mantra or formula) that seems appropriate. It is the perseverance in practice and faith in the Mantra that builds the one-pointed Vashana (habit energy) in the mind of the aspirant, not the power inherent in the Mantra itself. However, in India, it is felt that the teacher conveys his own spiritual power at initiation.

In the West, where Mantra meditation has become popular, newcomers are paying good sums of money for initiation with a Mantra. To the Indian scholar or adept this seems a dubious practice, as nobody owns the name of God. How can you sell what is not yours?

The following is an often quoted passage on Mantra, although the source is unknown.

"A Mantra is the natural name of an aspect of God (known as Devi or Devata) and is a syllable or syllables with power, revealed to Indian sages thru years of Yogic practice, meditation, and austerity. Moreover, when pronounced properly and used after true initiation by an enlightened teacher, a Mantra is equivalent to the Devi or Devata (God or Goddess) for which the name stands and carries all the power of that aspect of Divinity. For instance, an "Agni" Mantra invokes the power of fire*, Agni being the God, or essence, of fire.

"The aim of using Mantras is to purify and harmonize the vehicle of the Sadhaka (the practicer) so it may become increasingly sensitive to the subtle layers of his own

---

*Note: In this respect, there is an interesting story of a wondering Yogi who, passing thru a village, was asked if he would help prepare the refreshments (like vegetarian hors d'oeuvres) for a wedding celebration. He good-naturedly agreed, and while stuffing the refreshments, idly hummed a tune, which happened to be an Agni Mantra. The result? When the guests began sampling the hors d'oeuvres, they felt as though their throats and stomachs had been set aflame! Without meaning to do so, the holy man had invoked the Spirit of Fire,

consciousness. We purify the spiritual heart or nervous system and find the cosmos contained within.

"The basic doctrine underlying Mantra Shastra (doctrine) is that all this hard and tangible universe which we behold around us is made up only of different kinds of vibrations or energies working at various levels.

"The Indian Rshi (sage) says that all creation proceeds from sound (Nada) and the unheard sound (Para, or Vak) that is prior to vibration or manifestation, and that all vibration ultimately reduces to the sound OM, from which creation is supposed to have proceeded. The Yogi says that the universe is the result of an idea, and every idea is the result of sound.

"Mantra Yoga is that branch of Yoga in which the powers hidden in certain combinations of sound are utilized for the unfoldment of human consciousness. Each thing has a natural name which is the sound produced by the action of the moving forces which constitute it. He who mentally, or vocally, utters with creative force the natural name of any thing or any being brings to life whatever bears that name."

In other words, when we, thru meditation or concentration, use a Mantra of pleasing significance, in time we will actually become that which we have created. We become the object of our practice, and thus are the cognizer and cognized at the same time. This type of concept is, of course, difficult for the outgoing Western mind, but there is no doubt that we are influenced, even shaped, by that on which the mind dwells.

There is some dispute as to the importance pronuncia-

---

in much the same way that the great philosopher Sankara had done when, supposedly, he had caused flame to come from the palm of his hand to ignite the cremation of his mother on her death. Indians believe that a Mantra, in the hands of such a holy person, possesses great power.

tion plays in making Mantra practice efficient. Indian teachers usually insist on exact pronunciation of the Mantra, yet we do have the following instance to show that faith and perseverance may be more important:

The Sufis, who are said to represent the mystical arm of Islam, have long taught that one who repeats the sound "Hoo," or, more complete, "Yahoo," will derive great benefit. In this respect "Yahoo" could be called a Sufi Mantra. One time a great scholar came to a small village by a lake, and, hearing someone chanting this sound in a small hut, entered. "No, no, you've got it all wrong," he reproved the simple man who was sitting there practicing. "Let me teach you the correct pronunciation," he offered, and the simple practicer was delighted.

After a few minutes of instruction, the scholar left, walked down to the lake, and hired a boat to ferry him across. When the boat had been rowed to the center of the lake, the scholar looked back at the receding shore and noticed a man running to the lake shore from the hut he had just left. It was the simple practicer he had corrected. Then, to his amazement, he saw the man step onto the water and run across the surface of the waves until the man at last arrived at the boat holding the scholar! "Sir, I am so stupid," panted the man as he came running up, "I've already forgotten your instruction! Would you tell me again the correct pronunciation?"

This would seem to indicate that devotion and perseverance are powerful enough, even if the pronunciation is not correct. It is said that even the wrong means in the right hands will get results.

Another story will serve to demonstrate how the one chanting his own Mantra for years at a time, whether mentally or orally, will tend to become that to which he is devoted. There was a holy man (a Yogi) walking across

India, as is often the custom. He came to a temple and, going around to the rear, began to relieve himself against the wall. While walking, and while relieving himself, he never once stopped repeating the syllable "Ram," one of the names of God, for such was his practice.

One of the priests was highly displeased by this action, and came running over to the Yogi. "Don't you know better than to take the name of God while you are doing such a thing?" he demanded peevishly.

Surprised, the Yogi closed his mouth and stopped uttering the holy sound, but, immediately, every cell in the Yogi's body began shouting "Ram! Ram! Ram!"

Amazed, the priest shook his head. "Such restrictions are not for a man like you," he admitted in admiration. Literally, the Yogi and every cell of his body had turned into that to which he was devoted.

INSTRUCTION (Part One)

In India there are many techniques of using a Mantra. The first one we will study is the harmonizing of the Mantra "Ham-Sah" (or "So'ham," backward), Ham-Sah being the Divine Swan of Indian mythology.

In this meditation we are going to harmonize the two-syllabled Ham-Sah with the natural process of breathing.

Eyes closed, seated on a chair or in cross-legged position on the floor, mouth held shut and breathing thru the nose, with the tongue pressed against the palate (roof of the mouth), we begin. As we take a natural inbreath, we mentally repeat Ham; breathing out, we mentally repeat Sah. Some like to place these sounds in the third eye spot, between and slightly above the eyes, but it is not necessary.

Breathing naturally (no forcing or holding of breath), we repeat Ham-Sah for awhile. It may take days, or weeks, to build the Vashana (habit energy) of Ham-Sah, or it may happen immediately, but we will eventually begin to experience a period of Pure Consciousness (the Turiya State) during meditation. This means we will "lose" the Mantra and stop uttering it mentally; sights and sounds will disappear, and breathing will become almost imperceptible. All this will happen without volition, and it will be a period of "latent awareness," with no subject-object relationship, such as we usually experience. Literally, the world and we, ourselves, will temporarily disappear, as in a trance state. All this is accomplished without effort; we begin to repeat Ham-Sah mentally, in time with the breath, and the rest takes place naturally.

If we have performed the two Reverse Meditative Breaths first, it should be easy to quickly succeed with our Ham-Sah practice. Then we will experience a surcease from bodily and mental pressures; naturally, such relief will afford some healing benefits. There are also deeper spiritual rewards of which we may not be aware. Since many teachers, and the author, feel that, ultimately, all illness proceeds from a spiritual base, these "spiritual benefits" will certainly have an effect on health and chronic ailments. What do we mean by "spiritual?" Simply that which accords with *reality*, the opposite of *delusion*.

At first the experience of the Pure Consciousness (fourth state of consciousness) may appear to be "sleep," a sort of imageless sleep. As the mind becomes accustomed to it, however, and begins to enjoy it, we will note the difference. We are awake but not reacting; there is no conceptualization going on; all activity is in a latent state, and the tape recorder of the mind, with its eternal chattering, has been turned off.

A confirmed Yogi may well repeat this Mantra in rhythm with the breath all the time he is awake, but such practice is not for those of us who work in a busy world. After all, the Yogi is devoting his entire life to self-culture; we are simply adding one activity to our life to make it more fulfilling and meaningful.

After doing Ham-Sah for some months, we may notice one day that the process reverses. That is, unknowingly, we mentally repeat "Sah" (or "So") as we inhale and "Ham" as we exhale. The change can be made deliberately if it seems more natural to chant "So'ham" rather than Ham-Sah. "So'ham" literally means "That (the Reality) I Am," calling attention to the Divinity within the meditator. "So'ham" is considered a more advanced practice than "Ham-Sah," and some teachers in India say it is the way to acquire the Siddhis (supernatural powers). Both practices, repetition of Ham-Sah and repetition of So'ham, are well-known and highly regarded in India.

The author has experimented with repeating the two sounds in rhythm with the pulse (by placing one hand on the opposite wrist and noticing the pulse beat). Though he has never heard of this being done, it works very well. After all, the pulse beat has cosmic implications, too.

COMMENTARY

This practice of mentally repeating a Mantra is called "Manasika Japa." "Japa" means repetition of the formula that is the Mantra, orally, muttered, or mentally, as well as in writing. It is said that, in this, the decadent "Kali Yuga" of time, Japa, or remembrance of God's name, is the easiest and most proper practice to be followed for liberation. As we have shown, similar practices occur in other cultures under different names (such as the Japanese "Nembutsu" and the Sufi "Yahoo"). This would seem the time to consider what Japa is, and then to offer instruction in other modes of Japa.

There are many ways to "remember the Name," as Indian Japa is often described, but basically, we are going to deal with four.

The least known technique is that of "Likhita Japa," where one writes the Mantra a predetermined number of times, usually in the form of a lotus, a holy figure, or some other pleasing representation. This may be done 108 times, corresponding to the number of beads in a "mala" (Indian rosary), or some multiple of this number, such as 1080. The author had a student — a 76 year old woman, and a fine artist — who wrote the four lines of the Gayatri Mantra over and over in the shape of a sitting Buddha. It was a very appealing work of art, and also a good example of Likhita Japa. This "writing Japa" is very effective in silencing the mind and making it one-pointed in concentration on the Mantra. It is easy to read a page in a book without really comprehending what we have read, but when we write, we really have to concentrate on what we are doing. When the author has had to make a quick study of something, such as reading three or four texts in a day with the full intention of retaining what has been read, he has made it a practice to *write* syntheses of what he has learned, and then to write syntheses of the synthesis to compress it and register it in the mind. Writing is a wonderful way to focus on something.

The most common form of Japa in India is the audible chanting of a Mantra while fingering the 108 beads of the mala, so as to count to the predetermined number of repetitions. There are traditional rules for operating a mala (such as covering it with a towel, using the thumb and third finger exclusively, and not crossing the 108th bead, but reversing the progression), but they are not important to our purposes.

This process is call "Vaikhari Japa." Whether we count beads or do the oral Japa (with eyes open, often in company with others) a predetermined length of time, Oral Japa has all the benefits of chanting — we lose ourselves in it — and centers the mind on a sound, or sounds, we have found pleasing and believe to have great spiritual power.

Many of those who do Japa in India, whether in the temples or at home, do not chant the sounds aloud, but simply mutter them. One sitting nearby will not be able to determine what is being chanted, as there is little articulation. This is a combination of Oral and Silent Japa. Not as many do this form as do the Oral Japa, but often we find a holy man who spends his time muttering the name of God while wandering from place to place. This keeps the mind from darting here and there and centers it on one thought of great significance.

Manasika Japa, now becoming known in the Western world as "Transcendental Meditation,"* is as old as India and is difficult for some people to do, as it means repeating the Mantra mentally. Some like to "place" the Mantra in

*Note: In the effort to promote this form of Japa commercially, it has been said that "it has nothing to do with Yoga and nothing to do with religion." This is obviously ridiculous, as those making the claim well know. Practice with a Mantra is "Mantra Shastra," a very important field of Yoga and Tantric Yoga activity. Moreover, a Mantra is not just any sound; it is a Formula of Power revealed to an Indian sage, and corresponds to the name of God. The great modern-day saint, Swami Ramdas (who died some years ago), attained his enlightenment thru constant remembrance and chanting of the formula "Shri Ram Jay Ram Jaya Jaya Ram," his way of remembering the Divine. So we are working with a name of God, brought to us by a sage to whom it was revealed. If "revelation" and "remembrance of the name of God" is not religious, what is? Too much emphasis on commericalism, while enabling us to succeed in one direction, may cause us to fail in more important ways.

the third-eye spot, while others prefer to locate it just below the navel (haven't we all read of Yogis "contemplating the navel"?). Actually, while chanting the formula mentally in Manasika Japa, it will usually find its own location.

Unlike the practice of other forms of Japa, in Manasika Japa we keep the eyes closed. Whether we sit in cross-legged position or in a straight backed chair, repetition of the Mantra will build a big Vashana (habit energy) that will enable us, eventually, to reach the state of Pure Consciousness and abide there a little while before our tendencies (Samskaras) bring us back to the world of the senses. Becoming one-pointed in the mental sound, the miracle happens and we become "no-pointed," that is, all thinking disapppears and we are in the Turiya State, the unchanging fourth state of consciousness that underlies the others. The unutterable relief of continued and cumulative practice, when successful in achieving this state, cannot be described. It is highly effective in releasing stress of body and mind and, as such, is certainly healing to both. Achieving the egoless condition affords great benefit to the whole psyche and, as we become accustomed to this relief thru continued practice, we find we do not want to do without our daily meditation period. It represents a time of "recharging the batteries," and becomes the center from which our existence is renewed.

We say "period" rather than "periods" because we believe one late afternoon sitting of 45 minutes is more beneficial than two forced periods of 20 to 25 minutes each. When we arise in the morning the mind is usually dull and has great difficulty achieving the Turiya State. Moreover, we are usually rushing to get ready for work, with the mind full of plans for the day. It is a difficult time to do Japa and have it develop into deep meditation. On the other hand, in late afternoon, when the busy work day is over, we can usually relax (no cocktails or alcohol before meditation, however, as they will paralyze the nervous system!), do the Reverse Meditative Breaths, and then do a period of successful Manasika Japa. Even three-quarters of an hour may seem short when we are truly experiencing the fourth state of consciousness.

Manasika Japa should not be done at night before going to bed as it will probably prevent sleep. Actually, this state of pure consciousness is more restful than sleep itself. We tend to touch the Source in this practice.

While Japa, particularly Manasika Japa, is highly successful in reducing stress and relieving tensions, it is *not* a practice that directly affects the physical health in the way the Nei Kung or Moving Meditation (T'ai Chi Chih and T'ai Chi Ch'uan) do. The latter strongly circulate the vital force in the body. Indeed, if one does long periods of Manasika Japa, he should offset them with practice of Hatha Yoga, T'ai Chi Chih, or some other form which will start the intrinsic energy flowing again — otherwise there may be illness.

Manasika Japa, leading to the state of pure consciousness, should not be practiced for at least two hours after meals, and then a constant practicer should eat lightly. When the breath slows down and becomes barely perceptible, as happens in successful meditation of this kind, there is not enough oxygen being taken in to digest the food. This is an important point.

One teacher of Manasika Japa has pointed out that, if one uses the Mantra in this practice and does not succeed in entering the Pure Consciousness state, he is apt to have stomach trouble. It is easy to understand how this would be so with the Mantra "Ram," "Ra" being the sound associated with the digestive or gastric fire, but whether it would also apply to a different Mantra, such as the Gayatri, is a moot point.

Whether we use a mala (108 beads) or simply time our Oral Japa, we should try to perform it *at least* the predetermined number of times (or length of time) every day. In his fine book, *Japa Yoga*, Swami Shivananda, in great detail, tells us how many times we will have to repeat our formula to receive personal Darshan (meeting, interview) with the aspect of Divinity (god or goddess) invoked by the Mantra. This is not what we of the West are seeking, however.

The number of times we repeat the Mantra each day will obviously depend, to some extent, on whether we use a short Mantra (such as "Ram") or a lengthy one (such as "Hare Krishna Hare Krishna Krishna Krishna Hare Hare, Hare Rama Hare Rama Rama Rama Hare Hare" which is an offering to god Vishnu in the forms of his two Avatars, Rama and Krishna). If we determine to do 1080 repetitions of a lengthy Mantra, such as the above, or the Gayatri, we may use half the day doing them! It is better to be more conservative and choose some goal we can easily meet *every* day.

Once we have chosen a Mantra for Japa, or have been initiated with one, we stick with it the rest of our lives; there is no reason to switch. The great 15th Century Sufi Saint, Kabir, used "Ram" all his life, having been initiated with it by the great teacher of his time, Ramanuja.

INSTRUCTION (Part Two)

First we determine whether we are going to write our Japa, do oral repetitions, mutter our Mantra, or do Manasika (mental) Japa. In any case, regularity of practice will be a necessity, whether the benefits we are seeking are spiritual or physical or both.

If we want our Japa to develop into deep meditation, we should do Manasika Japa with the eyes closed. All Japa will relieve stress, but the bodily and mental relief experienced in the trance-like state to which Manasika Japa leads is much greater than that derived from the other forms.

We can sit cross-legged on the floor or comfortably in a chair to orally repeat our Mantra, or to mutter it. Eyes will be open, and we will be perfectly aware, at all times, of where we are. If we do Manasika Japa, we must be sure that our pose is well anchored so that we do not topple over and hurt ourselves during the thought-free period. Thus we must either sit in a chair or sit in Lotus position on the ground; the latter pose will tend to anchor us well and there will be no fears in our mind. Sitting cross-legged, without doing the Lotus, is not good enough for Manasika Japa unless we lean against a wall, affording us some support. With our eyes closed, we will probably go off into the state where we are not aware of what we are doing; the Mantra will take us along the path automatically.

Whichever form of Japa we do, we must have a Mantra with which to work. If one is fortunate enough to be initiated by an Indian Master, well and good. If not, the meditator can choose his own Mantra. The author suggests a sound such as "light" or "joy" for those who do not want to use a Hindu name of God. These two words have spiritual import, and one can build a meditation Vashana (habit energy) with them. Indeed, it is reported that the poet Tennyson succeeded in meditation by repeating his own name! Holding the mind to one thought is the basis of success, though initiation by a realized teacher can, admittedly, have a powerful effect.

Now, sitting in our chosen posture, with eyes closed (and, hopefully, having performed the Reverse Meditative

Breathings), we are ready to begin repetition of our Mantra in Manasika Japa.

One technique is to repeat the Mantra mentally with slow and even rhythm. Another technique, which is perhaps more effective, is to begin mental repetition of the Mantra as rapidly as possible (not being too concerned with the pronunciation), and it will gradually slow down and find its own natural pace. We are using the principle that is employed in pushing a boat out into a lake. As we push it, it floats out rapidly at first, then slows down and glides at an even tempo. Also, times when the meditation is not going well, we can speed up our mental repetitions, in effect making a new start. Sometimes this can be effective in overcoming any block.

After we have mentally repeated the sound or sounds for a while, there may ensue a period in which the Mantra gets "lost" and we are inactive, resting in Pure Consciousness. At first we may think we have been asleep. We come out of this imageless rest with some random thoughts having nothing to do with our meditation. After much practice, we will become aware of this quickly and immediately begin to repeat our Mantra again (which will probably take us "under" very quickly the second time). However, the beginning meditator may allow the mind to wander aimlessly for a while before realizing what is happening.

The rapid passage of time during this thought-free period will amaze the meditator at first. He is not aware of time going by, and may meditate for a longer period than he intended. The mind, feeling good, does not want to leave immersion. However, as he becomes at home with his meditation, he will be able to regulate it.

Success in Manasika Japa, that is, the entering of the thought-free state, may take some time for the beginner to achieve. Using the Reverse Meditative Breaths as a preliminary will make it much easier to achieve the Pure state of Consciousness, as the mind will be quieted even before the repetitions begin.

From a health standpoint, there is much more rest from a period of Pure Consciousness than from a period of dryly repeating the Mantra without losing it, where the sound persists and the meditator does not enter the Turiya State. However, even a continued mental repetition, without any semblance of trance state, is beneficial; it will correspond to a period of Oral or Muttered Japa.

COMMENTARY

All forms of repetition — written, oral, muttered, or mental — are beneficial. Japa will be more meaningful if one uses a sound of spiritual significance, but concentration on any one thought, to the exclusion of others, will achieve results.

It is Manasika Japa which turns into meditation. One must remember to do the mental repetitions in a quiet, relatively dark place where there will not be sudden noise such as a telephone or barking dog. The nervous system becomes extremely sensitive in deep meditation, and to be brought out of the immersion suddenly and violently will definitely not be healing. Except for this possibility, all meditation derived from Japa has salutary effects on the health. Particularly those with heart conditions, or with hypertension and high blood pressure, should find the complete rest of the thought-free period the best medicine they can have. With patience and regularity of practice, those with chronic ailments may find marked improvement and, what's more, achieve a contented frame of mind.

BREATH COUNTING (Breath-Dhyana)
There is another form of meditation that achieves

exactly the same results as Manasika Japa, that is, enables the meditator to enter the trance-like state of Pure Consciousness thru mental repetition. Here we do not repeat a name of God or holy formula; we simply breathe naturally and count either the inbreaths or outbreaths. This type of meditation is called "Breath-Dhyana"; the word "Dhyana" meaning "meditation" in the Sanskrit language. There is no devotion implied in this meditation. We are not "remembering the Name," nor are we dwelling on the "aspects of Divinity." We simply work with the physical mechanism, using the breath as our key to deeper states.

INSTRUCTION

It would be best to perform the Reverse Meditative Breathings three or nine times before beginning the Breath-Dhyana, thus stilling the mind and preparing it for immersion. Then, seated comfortably, with back straight, eyes and mouth closed, and tongue resting against the roof of the mouth, we begin to count either our inbreaths or outbreaths, but not both. If the count reaches ten, we then begin again at one. We do not want the mind to grapple with higher numbers, as they might be distracting, anchoring us to the counting. In effect, the numbers are simply tools, harnessed to the breath, and we want them to drop away naturally as the mind achieves the thought-free state. We breathe naturally, and may even notice, after the Reverse Meditative Breathings, that the breath has become so subtle that we can barely find it. This is a salutary sign. Nevertheless, there is always a slight rising and falling of the diaphragm, and this can generally be detected. Do not be surprised if you do not reach the number ten in your counting. Whether this success happens quickly, or whether it takes weeks of regular practice, as the mind gets used to the meditation it will become difficult even to get halfway to "ten." Then a period of immersion in pure consciousness will be experienced, with no activity. When thought begins again, one starts to count again. The meditator should not anticipate results; he should just proceed with his counting, as he would with the Mantra, and the results will happen by themselves.

Those who have studied in one particular tradition or another may argue that results are better when arrived at using the Mantra or technique of their own guru, but the thought-free state of Pure Consciousness is the same no matter which technique we use. We can swim across a lake, paddle a canoe, row a boat, or even fly, but in any case, we reach the other shore sooner or later. The choice of whether to use a Mantra or the Breath-Dhyana is entirely up to the meditator and his predilections.

COMMENTARY

Psychiatrists and psychologists should be particularly interested in these meditations that lead to the trance state as they afford the greatest amount of relief from stress and tension and are probably the easiest meditations to perform. One makes little continued effort, yet the Mantra or breath counting take over and lead the way to the "Promised Land." One psychologist the author knows — and has taught — suggests using a holy name taken from the religious background of the meditator, instead of the standard Mantra. This seems to attain the desired result. A Vashana (habit energy) is built with the name that has real meaning to the aspirant. For those who have no religious inclinations, the Breath-Dhyana will serve the same purpose. Cause leads to effect.

In our hectic world of today, where so much diversion

and so many stresses fight for the attention of the mind, there is usually real bifurcation of thought. One-pointed concentration is rare. Rather, the mind jumps incessantly from one fear, one hope, one plan, and one sense-stimulus to another, without surcease. When this type of meditation is regularly practiced, the mind — and body — receive incredible relief by laying down the burdens. Resting in complete abstraction, for a while, there is complete absence of strain. Can this help but be healing? Whether we believe that there are other benefits from this intimate contact with Reality or not, the rest derived from successful practice should be obvious to all.

Doctors, psychiatrists, and psychologists will, more and more, turn to meditation to help their patients in self-healing. Perhaps hypochondria will disappear, perhaps fears will be lessened, and perhaps the removal of stress will help the patient recover lost energy. It is important that the doctor caution his patient to follow the proper instructions implicitly, as given, and not go down strange byways, mixing other practices and theories with the simple teaching given here. Such practices as "Soul Travel" will lead to astral projection (leaving the body), and are very dangerous. This is not what we are looking for. We are studying meditation for healing. Professional men, please tell your patients and clients to follow directions carefully and not attempt to make a smorgasbord out of meditation. The meditations taught in this book for healing purposes are time-tested. They do not consist of simplistic aphorisms that make one feel good, in the way diversions do. If words spoken to us could do the trick, each one would walk out of Church, on Sunday, a changed person after hearing the sermon! Rather, the Mantra Meditations or the Breath-Dhyana should be done without preconcept. The benefits will follow of their own accord.

Chapter 7
THE WAY OF MINDFULNESS
Instruction and Commentary

Now we come to the "Way of Mindfulness" ("Satipat-thana" in Indian languages), the Buddha's great meditation that directly led to his all-encompassing enlightenment 2500 years ago. Only one man in historical times has been called "Buddha," meaning "Fully Enlightened One." Other epithets have been coined to show the Buddha's perfection, such as "Tathagata" (He Who Thus Comes), and "Bhagavan" (Lord). It must be remembered that the Buddha was not born with this great enlightenment, nor did he claim he was a god, or that he received "Divine Revelation." A Prince of the Shakya country in northwest India, he left his wife and child, as well as his patrimony (which would have made him King), out of compassion for the suffering of all beings, and became a wandering mendicant in order to achieve enlightenment and to use it for the benefit of all. After almost starving to death, he reached his goal under the Bodhi Tree (at BodhiGaya), emerging from the four meditative absorptions to the full realization of life everywhere, in all possible worlds. It is said that he sat immersed in bliss for 49 days before being persuaded (by the god Brahma) to use his great attainment for the benefit of all beings.

Among the Buddha's postulations, based on his deep

experience, was the Noble Eight-Fold Path, and mindfulness is the first of the seven "Factors of Enlightenment" as taught by the Buddha. From this it can be seen how important mindfulness is on the path to perfection.

As a meditation, the Satipatthana encompasses more than any of the others we talk about in this book. It is a complete psychological system of self-discovery, and its power will make an impact on the practicer's life 24 hours of the day.

At first our practice of the Satipatthana will be performed at regular sittings (cross-legged or in a chair), with this exception: we will be asked to frequently scrutinize our posture and our state of mind during the day, not to correct them in any way, but just to be aware of them.

So much of our busy life is lived unconsciously. While we wash our teeth, we are daydreaming; when shaving, we are making plans, and often do not remember afterward whether or not we have shaved. And when we do remember, how much we add to the memory, embellishing the bare facts until they are unrecognizable! Zen says, "When eating, there should be only the eating. When thinking, there should be only the thought," and adds, "When hungry we eat, when tired we sleep." Isn't this what we all do? No, a thousand times no! When eating we do not even taste because the mind is wandering. And one thought leads endlessly to other thoughts, beginning long chains of association that end in attachment and clinging, bringing misery in their wake. In this unknowing way we create our Karma, the inevitable reactions that follow actions, and resulting in ill health, among other things. When Krishnamurti speaks of "choiceless awareness," he means perception without reaction, just being aware of what is happening. To experience such awareness, we must be temporarily motiveless, whereas the panting heart, full of wishes and desires, running after every desirable object, sees everything thru a screen of self-interest.

The Satipatthana encourages, even forces, awareness of what is happening inside as well as in the world around. We simply note it, without condemnation or approval. If the mind finds it "pleasing," we make a note of such; that's all. And yet, within the four categories (which gradually contract to become one all-enveloping classification), all things are included — our thoughts, reactions, and sensations.

After a while, our regular "sittings" in Satipatthana become almost unneccessary. We are doing the meditation all the time.

This is not a meditation that will lead to trance-states. It will greatly enhance our feeling of "here and now," as we unavoidably learn what makes us tick, what tricks the mind plays, and how we *really* react to the world each day and night. It may change our mistaken self-image. In short, it does away with delusion and illusion.

"Bare Awareness" is the foundation of the Satipatthana, and it is a completely new approach for most of us. Whether we are seeking merely the healing effects of such an all-encompassing mediation, or whether we welcome the enlightening effects that come with it, there is no more beneficial practice we can follow.

We begin practice by watching our state of mind and becoming aware of our posture, without correcting it, during the day and night. Soon we notice that there is a definite relationship between the two. It is easy to see how the state of mind affects the posture; the harrassed man hurries around all bent over without being aware of it. It is a little more difficult to realize that the way we sit, stand,

and walk will affect our attitude and state of mind. Zen practice puts the greatest emphasis on posture during Zazen (Zen "sitting" or meditation) and, in a temple, a monk walks around with a big stick called the "Keisaku" to make sure the sitter remembers to sit properly! It is an apt reminder. Zen says that, when you are slumped over, you are probably daydreaming; Zen practice is an exercise in "nowness." Obviously much of Zen, in the early days, was derived from the Satipatthana, the "Way of Mindfulness." A brief story might illustrate this:

After studying with his Zen Master fifteen years, a Zen monk was given full approval (Inka) and allowed to go out on his own to teach. Returning to visit his master one rainy day, he placed his umbrella and wooden clogs (the Japanese do not wear rubbers to keep out the water, they walk over it on clogs) neatly on the floor in the anteroom before entering the room where his master was waiting.

"Did you place your umbrella on the right side of your clogs or on the left?" was the master's greeting to his visitor.

Thunderstruck, the new teacher tried desperately to remember, and could not do so. He had lost his "24-hour awareness," so vital in Zen. As a result, he gave up his own students and returned to study with his old master ten more years!

This is a dramatic excursion into the meaning of "true awareness." Not all of us are aiming at Zen enlightenment, though it might not be a bad idea, but our health and well-being depend, to a considerable extent, on whether we are the master of ourself or just a piece of flotsam tossed aimlessly hither-and-yon.

INSTRUCTION

As a preliminary, at intervals during the day, we are to

watch our posture and our state of mind; in the beginning, the latter may be more difficult to determine than is supposed. Then, when we are ready to commence formal sittings, we take our seat (cross-legged or in a chair) and spend a length of time (10 minutes, perhaps) on *each* of the following four categories:

1. MINDFULNESS OF THE BODY. We watch the rise and fall of the diaphragm in breathing, thus becoming mindful of the body. We breathe naturally without counting the breaths. The diaphragm rises and falls; we are breathing, or being breathed. Sometimes it is a long breath, sometimes it is a short one. As the teachers say, "If it is a long breath, so be it. If a short breath, well and good." We change nothing; we are just aware of our breathing. And during the day we note our posture, being mindful of the body in this way.

2. MINDFULNESS OF SENSATION. Now we turn our attention (for another ten minutes) to the sensations, inner and outer, we experience. Noting the feel of the backside touching the chair, we become aware of a slight sourness in the stomach. A light breeze touches the cheek, and we note it. All sensation or feeling is merely noted.

And each time we are aware of a sensation, we also make a note of whether the reaction is pleasant, unpleasant, or merely neutral. This is how the mind works; it classifies. Therefore, we watch it classifying. Doing this, one day we may have the sudden insight that thoughts have a life of their own; we watch them and realize "we" are not the thoughts. This will make quite an impact.

3. MINDFULNESS OF THE STATE OF MIND. This is the most difficult of the four categories. For about ten minutes we introspect our state of mind, which is constantly shifting. A motorcycle makes a loud noise outside, startling us, and we note: "mind with annoyance."

We become restless, feeling that the meditation will never end, and we merely make a note: "impatient mind." We may even wonder whether all this practice has any meaning, so we note: "doubting mind." Nothing escapes us. And we try to watch our state of mind during the day, along with our posture. It is a practice that really leads to nonattachment, even to our own thoughts and moods.

4. OBJECTS OF MIND. We sit another ten minutes practicing this most inclusive category. This is closest to Zen practice, and appeals more than the other categories to those of intellectual bent.

Actually, all perceptions and all thoughts are "objects of mind." We hear a noise outside, and we note it. Seeing the rug in front of us, we are consciously mindful of it. A sudden memory flashes thru the mind, and we observe it. If we consider the mind as the "sixth sense" in Buddhist fashion, then whatever comes to us thru the senses is an "object of mind." It is not easy to make a note of every perception, let alone thought, but, with practice, we will be able to do so.

It will be noted that number 2 — "Mindfulness of Sensation" — and number 4 — "Objects of Mind" — overlap somewhat. In combined practice we will make these one, not only noting the sensations, but the sense perceptions and thoughts as well and, each time, noting if the reaction is pleasing, displeasing, or neutral.

COMBINED PRACTICE. Having become familiar with the four categories separately, we now will seek to combine them in the real Satipatthana practice. We will sit 40 minutes, or an hour.

Our basic focus will be on the breath, the rising and falling of the diaphragm, and we will come back to it each time there is, temporarily, no other Mindfulness operating.

Sitting watching the breath, and being aware of the posture, the mind is ready to receive any other impression. A thought comes, and we note it as "objects of mind" and, since it stimulates the mind quite a bit in this instance, we look at the state of mind, which we find to be one of expectancy. "Expectant mind" or "eager mind" we note. A draft from the window sends a chill thru our system, and we note the feeling and the fact that it is unpleasant. Who was fool enough to leave the window open? We make a note: "mind with resentment" — our feeling toward the unknown perpetrator. We have decided, in advance, to sit for one hour, but only fifteen minutes have passed and we are beginning to be uncomfortable. Making a note of the discomfort and the fact that it is "displeasing," we slightly shift our position, feeling guilty that we are doing so: "mind with guilt." Then back to watching the breath rise and fall, our basic meditation.

And so it goes, never stopping. Eventually we will carry out these categories automatically night and day — and they may influence our dreams as well. Regular sittings are helpful, but the Satipatthana meditation goes on all the time.

COMMENTARY

The effects of Satipatthana practice are startling. For the first time we see how we actually operate; for the first time we have self-knowledge. This meditation, in the beginning, can hit one like a bombshell. One student of the author's declared that, suddenly, he saw his whole life going by in front of his eyes like a speeded-up newsreel! Big changes were to shortly take place in the student's life.

Psychologically, all sorts of unconscious neurosis may disintegrate with this practice. The author has heard students tell how their allergies all disappeared, and their fears, too. A strong realization of impermanence may be gained; unwillingness to recognize this impermanency is a great source of suffering. We may even become aware of our own disagreeableness, our sudden moods, and our constant judgment of everything that occurs. One Gestalt psychologist who studied with the author says he is now using the Satipatthana in his practice. It would seem to have great validity in the fields of psychiatry and psychology.

This meditation helps to heal the sick mind. Delusion brings craving, followed by jealousy or hatred in some form, so relief from delusion is greatly to be desired. The author believes the Satipatthana, in many ways, is the "King" of meditations, and completely practical for our mundane everyday lives. Accordingly, it is probable that all prospective meditators will find something of value in it, even if they intend to concentrate on other meditations.

Chapter 8
FIXATION — CHIH K'UAN
Instruction and Commentary

The Chih-K'uan meditation of Chinese T'ien T'ai Buddhism is one of the author's favorites. Simple in execution, it is profound in effect. Faithfully practiced, it is capable of bringing one to sudden insights that can change lives, even to the "Satori" (sudden enlightenment) experience.

T'ien T'ai has evolved a complicated metaphysics of healing, but this would require lengthy study on the meaning of Void, or Emptiness (Shunyata) in Buddhism, and it is not our purpose to spend too much time on the theoretical; we want to encourage the meditator to practice, not philosophize. However, some background in the philosophy as it relates to the healing of illness might be helpful.

There is nothing which does not change, so there is no permanence. What is not permanent is, ultimately, not real. Buddhism says that the transitory is simply a transformation, as the seed becomes the tree, the tree becomes timber, and the timber becomes ashes. Even names and forms of impermanent things are not real. So what we see, what we feel, and what we think is really empty — empty of any enduring self-nature. Thus we contemplate the Void, or Emptiness of Things.

Then we shift our contemplation to the world of phenomena, which T'ien T'ai knows as the "seeming." Although the nature of mind is empty (Void) as we now know, still, conditioned by circumstances and Karma, it can produce all the things of the world, including ourselves. So, knowing full well that these perceived things are, at bottom, empty, still we see the mountains and rivers and have thoughts. Knowing the true nature (which is no-nature) of things is empty, we, for the first time, really perceive the green of the grass and the brightness of the stars. There is no attachment to cloud our vision.

However, we do not stop there. We have realized all things as empty, yet we do see and feel the phenomena of the world. The two together — the Empty and the Phenomenal — are but symbols, arrows pointing to the Mean. Then we can truly live in this empty, phenomenal universe, playing our role in what is essentially a show of phantoms. We do not take "nay" as answer, and we do not take "yea." Knowing the Mean, we perceive Truth and can live our lives meaningfully as both common men and sages.

This much has been explained in rudimentary fashion, but it can be seen that such contemplation demands a deep and dedicated mind. So we overlook the philosophy, which is admittedly healing to the body and spirit, and proceed to instruction in the actual Chih-K'uan meditation.

INSTRUCTION (Part One)

Seating ourselves in either cross-legged position or in a chair, we concentrate intently on one spot in the body. We choose either the Tan T'ien below the navel (usually the most difficult), the tip of the nose, or the "third-eye" spot slightly above and between the eyes. This is our thought, this intense concentration, and such fixation is called "Chih."

Although, theoretically, we can have only one thought at a time, and our intense thought is concentration on the spot in the body, in actual practice the mind tends to wander. There is nothing wrong with this, it is natural in the beginning, but it is important to realize we are wandering and bring the mind back to the point of concentration. However, if the thoughts become heavy and frequent, as they probably will, we drop the intense concentration and just watch the thoughts as though we are watching a parade; we do not identify with them. This is "K'uan." Where did the thoughts come from? Where are they going? We just watch them without in any way attempting to analyze or alter them. When we watch our thoughts in this manner, without getting caught up in them, they will disappear. Then we return immediately to the "Chih," the basic concentration on a chosen spot in the body.

Although it sounds exceedingly simple to do Chih-K'uan, it is hard to make the mind conform to such a pattern for long unless we are really diligent. In ordinary Chih-K'uan practice, the teachers tell us first to breathe deeply, visualizing all our infirmities as being expelled thru all the pores in our body as we breathe out. We can even inhale thru the sex organ, expand the breath to fill the entire body, and then breathe out thru every pore as we throw out all illness. However, it would be preferable to do the Reverse Meditative Breathings first, as they are really helpful and will still the wandering mind before we even start our meditation. Under these circumstances, results should really be good if we practice regularly for 30 or 45 minutes at a time.

COMMENTARY

Before instructing the reader in a variation of this Chih-K'uan meditation, we want to say a word about the "Amitabha" sect of Buddhism (called "Amida" in Japan) so the reader will understand what we are dealing with.

Aeons ago a great spiritual aspirant (Bodhissatva, an enlightened being on his way to becoming a Buddha) named "Dharmakara" took 48 great vows, the most important of which was a vow to "Save all Sentient Beings." If Dharmakara became a Buddha, he promised that anyone, no matter how weak or how sinful, who remembered his name at least ten times would be taken, at death, to the "Western Paradise," the "Pure Land," where conditions would be ideal for practice, and the weakest one would, in time, become a Buddha and realize Nirvana. This Bodhisattva became the "Buddha of Infinite Light" ("Amitabha" in India and China, and "Amida" in Japan), and his vow is still in force today. Consequently, if the one who chants his name in remembrance only believes in the Buddha of Infinite Light, his eventual salvation is assured. Note that the Buddha does not judge; he has compassion for all sufferers, the sinner and saint alike.

The reasoning behind this religious practice, now so popular in Japan, is simple. Most of us in this decadent age are weak and do not have the determination or staying power to reach Nirvana by our own efforts; therefore, we depend on the "Other Power" for salvation. After all, we are sentient beings, too, and the Buddha's saving vow, still in force, includes us with the others. Unlike the exhortation of the historic Gautama Buddha, who said to "work out your own salvation diligently!" we are going to depend on the strength of Amitabha's vow, knowing he will save us.

This practice, of course, is an excellent way to nullify the ego-sense and to merge in something stronger than ourselves, whether we call it "Jesus" or "Amitabha."

INSTRUCTION (Part Two)

We close our eyes and concentrate intently on one of the three centers in the body — the forehead, the nose, or below the navel.

Then we mentally call out: "Amitabha! Amitabha!" Something echoes in the mind, and we listen. Where did the sound come from? Who uttered it? Who is hearing it?

In this variation of the basic meditation, we are creating our own thought deliberately, the thought of Amitabha, Buddha of Infinite Light. When we introspect the thought, or silent sound, in the manner above, the name will disappear and the mind will, for the moment, be totally silent. Then we return to our basic meditation, the intense concentration on one of the body spots.

COMMENTARY

If we were able to continue concentration on the body spot for the whole period of meditation (Chih), we would not need the K'uan part of the practice. In one of his classes, when the students had performed the Chih-K'uan meditation for just 15 minutes, the author was surprised when one student insisted that he had had no intervening thoughts for the whole period of time, and so just continued his fixation (Chih). The author assured him that, if this were really so and he was able to practice this efficiently often, an eventual insight experience of great depth (Satori) would probably come his way!

Many realizations as to the meaning of Impermanence and Ultimate Emptiness should come to one who practices Chih-K'uan faithfully. The mind will then feel fresh and vigorous, the body light and healthy. This stillness of meditation and intense concentration, leading to one-pointedness, are, of course, very helpful to those suffering from stress and strain; such concentration leads to great relief from tension.

Chuang-Tzu, the great Chinese Taoist philosopher, often wrote of the "fasting mind," the mind that gradually pares away the unneccessary rather than piling up continued mental debris. This is difficult for most of us, for we form great attachments. Yet it is the only way we can remain with the natural as opposed to the artificial, and function spontaneously instead of out of blind habit.

In Buddhism, true "fasting" means doing without greed, anger, and delusion; these are the three that bring suffering, and are at the base of all illness. Practice of Chih-K'uan will help us to attain this "fasting mind," and can remake us mentally and physically. Do not underestimate the effects of this "simple" meditation!

Chapter 9
VISUALIZATION —
TIBETAN DUMO HEAT
Instruction and Commentary

The author has promised to let the reader know a bit about his experience in developing the Tibetan "Dumo Heat" that is so overpowering. Many, including doctors, have asked such questions as whether this practice raises the body temperature. In order to understand the building of the Dumo Heat, however, it is probably necessary to throw away Western "scientific" concepts and view it all from the standpoint of age-old Eastern practices. Only in this way will one be able to grasp the significance and possibility of the meditator progressing to a point where the vital force flows thru the central meridian channel of the body to an extent that the physical mechanism becomes almost impervious to cold. It will be even more difficult to realize that, despite certain physical practices, such a culmination will be largely the result of thought and visualization. The theory may be difficult to grasp; the experience, be assured, is very real.

Actually, it was many years ago in the Himalayan foothills that the author's interest was first aroused. Living among the holy men, he saw them bathing in the Ganges at 4 a.m. every morning, regardless of the freezing temperature. Monkeys, burros, other animals, even occasionally elephants gathered on the narrow banks of the river at that hour and often bathed together. The holy men were included. All was peaceful, unless the roar of a tiger was heard, and then everyone scattered, with the monkeys sometimes fainting!

In spite of the cold, the holy men usually wore only a string around the loins, and few carried towels. Those who have read of Tibetan Yogis melting the snow for many feet around them with the heat of their nude bodies will not be too surprised. There is one test, in Tibetan Yogic practice, where the initiate must dry soaking-wet towels by draping them on his body.

The author saw holy men meditating while lying in water, and was told that they were working with the "Kundalini" force. Because of the tremendous heat generated, they were forced to immerse themselves during practice so that their nervous systems would not be burned out. Such occurrences are not just idle fancy. The power of a mastery of Prana (Chi, Shakti, Kundalini) is so great that the sage, Sri Aurobindo, declared: "With complete mastery of it, one would be able to build another Universe!"

When we are "sick," the body automatically generates heat (fever) which serves a very special purpose in purification. However, it is the usual Western practice not to seek the cause, but to take drugs to dissipate the heat so laboriously produced by the body; that is, lower the fever. However, in the secret Nei Kung, in the Moving Meditations (T'ai Chi Chih and T'ai Chi Ch'uan), and in the circulation of the Dumo Heat, an intense warmth is deliberately created in the body. This warmth results from the circulation of the vital force thru the meridian channels, and it is very healing. Even in the "laying on of hands" and "Johrei," the recipient usually notices great heat, and this heat is healing in nature.

One time the author had a student in T'ai Chi Chih, the Moving Meditation, who was just recovering from an auto accident. His right eye was partly closed by injury to the right side of his head. The very first night of T'ai Chi Chih class, as he began to experience the flow of the Chi, a strong fever developed in the affected side of his face. Gradually the eye began to open. By the time the seventh lesson (three weeks later) was reached, the eye had returned to normal. He was delighted, and asked for an explanation, particularly of the sudden fever that arose as the Chi was flowing. The author explained that the Chi energy flowed freely unless there was blockage, in which case it would turn into intense heat in much the same way that electricity, flowing freely, turns into electric light when it is properly interfered with.

The heat from the flow of the vital force, brought on by either mental or physical activity, or both, seems capable of extraordinary healing activity. At a recent Teachers' Training Course, one student with a third degree burn on her hand began to develop a pleasing warmth in the sore area, over and above the warmth of the burn itself, and the rapidity of scar-free healing was amazing. There have been numerous such incidents demonstrating the healing effects of this Yin Chi, Yang Chi practice. The movements and concentration have, as expected, caused heat, and the healing results have been most often observed in cases of chronic illness or injury.

INSTRUCTION

Without comment, the author will recount some of the practices he followed in developing this Dumo Heat ("Dumo" referring to the great channel in the front of the body, known as "Tumo" to the Chinese).

Each morning, before leaving for work, the author did

both his Moving Meditations and Zazen, accompanied by chanting. Returning home in the afternoon, he again did one of the Moving Meditations, followed by a Hatha Yoga practice known as "Udiyana," in which the Prana is forced from the lower abdomen up the Central Channel, aided by contraction of the anus and action of the legs. The legs were spread apart, and the trunk of the body was slightly bent over, with the two hands placed backward on the two thighs, hands and fingers spread wide.

This Yoga Asana was followed by various breathing exercises: ordinary Pranayama (in which first one and then the other nostril is covered), with progressively longer times in which the breath was held, the "Joyous Breath" of T'ai Chi Chih, the two Reverse Meditative Breathings, and a mental routing of the Chi thru the eight main channels of the body (splitting into two at the belt, going up the outside of the back, down the outer arms and across the key middle finger, up the inside of the arms from the palms). This was usually performed nine times. Certain Taoist practices with the thumbs, some massage, rubbing of the upper and lower lips, and other movements were executed, all designed to raise heat. The final few times the author took the Chi thru the eight channels, he began by inhaling thru the sex organ and exhaling, mentally casting off all impurities, thru every cell in the body.

All these were considered preliminary practices. The real work began when the author seated himself in meditation at the open door (no matter how cool the weather) and began his visualizations. The sitting posture was the one used in Zazen.

The Tibetans counsel the practicer to visualize his body as entirely empty, then to mentally "see" the central channel (the Sushumna, red-and-white) and the two outside channels, as in the second of the Reverse Meditative

Breathings. The three channels wound downward from the eyes to the spot between the legs.

Then the author rolled spittle around in the mouth (keeping the tongue pressed against the palate) and, along with the breath, swallowed the spittle, taking it sharply down to the Tan T'ien below the navel, as the anus was contracted; after a pause, the air (and Chi) was forced up thru the central channel in four sections, after first rolling the stomach several times in a circular manner. The air from the contracted anus was forced upward (with what is called "Apanna") to meet the air and Prana being swallowed in the Tan T'ien, where they mixed before the stomach was rotated and the mixture forced up thru the central channel.

Sometimes the author varied this last practice by an invention of his own, which he called the "Earth-Sky" meditation. Here the Yang vibration of the sky would be taken in thru the head (the way the warm golden light from the waterfall is in the first part of the Great Circle Meditation) and brought down to the space below the navel; the Yin vibration of the earth was brought up thru the soles of the feet, and the two forces met at the Tan T'ien. One can also practice this by lying nude on the earth, in the sunshine, drawing up the Yin vibration thru the body cells and mixing it with the Yang of the sunshine soaking in above. The reader will easily understand the point-in-common with these different versions of the same practice.

Now, sitting with fists on knees, in cross-legged position, the author began his visualizing meditation. Though Tibetan instruction tells us to bring a white dot (the "Bindu," the essence of the semen) down from the forehead, the author, instead, pictured a duck's egg on top of his head, dripping nectar down thru the skull as in the first part of the Great Circle Meditation (after rising on the cloud to the base of the waterfall). This nectar was to be brought down to mingle with the fire rising from between the legs, the most important part of the practice.

First the author would, mentally, take the Chi around the Tan T'ien, making a circle nine times; then, having circled counter-clockwise, he would reverse the circle clockwise. When finished, he would visualize a thin tongue of flame (the Tibetans say "brown flame," but this is not important) between the legs, extending up thru the center of the body (not the front or back), and looking somewhat like the Tibetan written 'A' . The thin point (indicated by the arrow) would gradually straighten; it was extremely hot. Then, with the anus contracting progressively tighter (in vibrating waves), the author would gradually bring this heat up (the tongue of flame lengthening) as the nectar from the duck's egg came down to meet it at the spot below the navel. Mentally, the author repeated an Indian Mantra with "Ra" as its base, for "Ra" is the sound governing that part of the body and affecting the gastric heat in the lower digestive regions.

As the tongue of flame lengthened and came up to meet the descending nectar, with the author mentally repeating the Mantra and contracting the anus, the flame would grow hotter and expand to the outlying cells of the lower body. Occasionally the author would roll the stomach violently (one must not be full of food while doing these practices!), still contracting the anus. At this point perspiration would usually burst forth.

Eventually the brightening flame would engulf all the cells of the body below the heart level. A real heat would be felt, but it was sporadic and would come and go quickly.

COMMENTARY

For about a year, with occasionally a few days respite, these and other practices would be faithfully carried out. Friends wondered why the author was never available for dinner invitations; his financial associates of the mornings did not suspect his double life.

Each Thursday the author attended a Zazen session at the apartment of a dedicated Zen woman. At the start of the session one very cool winter Thursday evening, the author threw himself into his own practices with great energy. Soon the room began to turn warm; the author wondered if the heat had been turned on. Little by little, as joyous energy started to flood his body, he began to feel as if he was literally burning up. At the finish of the sitting, before tea was served, the author blurted out some explanation to his astonished hostess and quickly left. Arriving home, he sat on an upright chair, feeling as though all the "faucets" inside him had been turned on. After resting quietly for a long time, just feeling the incredulous flow, he opened the windows wide (the temperature was in the 30's) and went to bed, using just a light cover. Soon even this was too much and, lying nude under just a sheet, the author gave himself up to the joyous flows that were tumbling thru his body. Burning in temperature and wide awake from the energy, he found sleep to be impossible. Eight hours passed in this manner. The author was afraid he would be too tired to work the next day; actually, in the morning, he was flooded with energy.

What is strange is that during this time of the cascading energy, there were no psychic experiences, no visions such as he had seen at other times. There was just the joyous coursing of energy thru the channels of the body, arousing heat that seemed to make one oblivious of the cold and to leave one in a euphoric condition.

The following morning, the author had to make a decision as to whether he would pay the price to continue the amazing flow (which would have made work almost impossible) or to let the energy gradually subside and, having achieved the goal briefly, not to continue the practice. The author decided on the latter course of action, confident in his ability to recapture the great flow if he decided to devote himself to it again in the future. It must be remembered that the Yogis in the Himalayas devote *ALL* their time to their practices; they do not work for a living.

Such experiments are not recommended for meditators. Yet there is much to be learned from such experiences, and the author feels they carry the germ of great healing practices.

CLOSING COMMENTARY

In Tibetan Tantra and Chinese Taoism there is a method of recycling the sex energy. It is known as the "Backward Flowing Method," and it develops a powerful healing force. The author first discovered this for himself during one of his "difficult" periods while practicing the Dumo Heat meditation. It must be remembered that he was working every day in financial circles from 7 a.m. to 2 p.m., then living the isolated life of a Yogi until almost midnight. There came a time when, beset by intermittant internal bleeding and weak from other adverse effects, his energy dropped to a level where he could barely drag himself around. At the lowest point, as though remembering something, he walked to his meditation cushion and, seating himself in Zazen fashion, began to indulge in the most sensual sexual thoughts possible. This gradually brought a physical excitation, and then, eyes closed and back held straight, he took this energy from below the navel, thru the legs, and up to the top of the head, as in the Great Circle Meditation, part of the Reverse Meditative Breaths. Within fifteen minutes he felt an incredible change. The sex energy was turned into a healing force, and all the fatigue and weakness of the body "magically" disappeared. This is a great secret of healing, and one that will probably be scoffed at by unthinking doubters.

One time the author instructed a young financial counselor, over long distance phone, in this technique. The young man was recovering from a severe case of flu, he said, and seemed unable to regain his strength. Many have had this same experience in the aftermath of illness.

Following the author's telephone directions, using the transmuted sex energy, he was able to effect a complete recovery by the following day! In such instances a strong internal heat is generated, and that heat is certainly revivifying.

It is not advised that the average person attempt to raise this Dumo Heat unless he is willing to reduce his food intake and to allow little of an extraneous nature to enter his thoughts. We must understand the meaning of the reciprocal nature of Mind and Prana (thought and energy), and also know the principles of movement that engender

---

Note: It must be emphasized that the author had no teacher, no guru, on this adventure. Consequently, there may be many flaws in the methods he used, which were derived from Yogis he had met and from his reading.

One Yogi, who in particular impressed him, followed Tibetan practices that were extreme, and he had written a book about them, which nobody seemed to want. This Yogi showed the author a sequence of twenty pictures taken by an automatic camera set-up over a period of three hours while the Yogi was in deep Samadhi. By the tenth frame, light was beginning to issue from his body. From the fifteenth picture on, the body had disappeared; there was just an intense white light with no sign of any form!

the flow, balancing the Chi, in order to use such methods. For the ordinary person, the Moving Meditations and the Nei Kung are relatively easy ways to get such results. The extraordinary person, interested in more dramatic healing effects, may be intrigued by the author's experiences related above.

Skeptical, the author asked Professor Wen-Shan Huang whether such photos could be faked. The good professor shook his head, adding that a similar incident had happened when a great T'ai Chi Ch'uan master had been photographed in Taiwan while demonstrating that Moving Meditation. When the pictures were developed, a light bluish stream of light was seen to be coming from the spot below the navel. The author has had similar experiences in connection with T'ai Chi, though not as startling.

Perhaps, one day, use of the vital force, and the related sex energy, will be truly understood and everybody will be capable of using them for healing benefits.

Chapter 10
CHANTING
Instruction and Commentary

There are innumerable types of chanting, and the practice is very strong and beneficial, whether we chant in Latin (Gregorian Chants), in Sanskrit, in Chinese, in Tibetan, or in Japanese. Generally we chant in groups, gaining strength from others in the assemblage. The author, when doing "walking chanting" of the Heart Sutra in Zen temples, has felt as though the right side of his head was splitting and coming off; yet, though painful, it was not an unpleasant sensation. It is not even important that we understand the semantic meaning of what we are chanting. We *become* the chanting, and therefore lose our ego-selves.

In Tibet, monks — and laymen — not only chant the "Om Mani Padme Hum" (the "Jewel in the Lotus"), but also incessantly turn prayer wheels that have this great Mantra written on them. Anyone who has heard the deep bass chanting in a Tibetan temple has probably been thrilled by it and, when it is supplemented by the sounds of the ultra-long bass trumpets, it becomes a subconscious force of great power.

In China there are those who, every day, chant the great Mantra of Avalokitesvara Bodhisattva (Essence of Compassion): "Gate Gate Paragate Parasamgate Bodhi Svaha!" The translation of this is "Gone, Gone, Gone to the other shore . . ." but the author feels that an explanation of the meaning of the words of a Mantra will only serve to weaken its power. It is not a rational statement, but an irresistible formula. In China and Japan they chant a transliteration of this Mantra, as the sounds do not fit into pronunciation suitable for Japanese and Chinese. It becomes: "Gyate Gyate Hara Gyate Hara So Gyate Bodhi Svaha Ka Hanya Shin Gyo." In fact, the whole Heart Sutra ("Hridaya" in India; "Hanya Shin Gyo" in Japanese and Chinese, meaning the "kernal" or "essence" of the Prajna Paramita Scriptures) is transliterated, not translated, so it would be hard for anyone who had not studied it to grasp its profound meanings just by listening to it. When rendered in English it seems to lose some of its power, although certainly easier to understand.

In India, all holy men chant "Om," or "Aum," as it is sometimes pronounced. This is called the "Pranava," the sound that is the substratum of all creation. All things supposedly reduce to this one great primordial sound.

The author has had the experience of coming out of deep meditation and hearing, underneath, a rumbling "Om" as the base of the meditation, though he was not using this Mantra as his meditative technique. Actually, no one living in the every day world — a householder as he is called in India — should chant "Om," as it is a renunciate's Mantra. If one busy in the world were to chant "Om" regularly, it is felt that he would soon lose interest in his family, probably lose his job and his money, and would be drawn to the life of a recluse. Groups are to be cautioned against a prevalent practice of chanting "Om."

Just as sacred in India, however, is the "Gayatri" Mantra, a hymn to the sun containing the sounds of Creation, "Bhuh Bhuvah Svah," or "Earth, Sky, and Heaven." It is said that the Gayatri is appropriate for anybody, in any circumstances, and it is a delight to chant, whether it is sung, spoken, or meditated on mentally. The words of the Gayatri are:

    OM BHUH BHUVAH SVAH
    TAT SAVITUR VARENYAM
    BHARGO DEVASYA DHIMAHI
    DHIO YOO NAH PRACHODAYAT

When we sing, rather than chant, the Gayatri sounds like this:

Om Bhuh Bhu-vah Sva-ha Tat Sav-it-ur Var-en-yam Bhar-go De-

vas-ya Dhi-ma-hi-i Dhi-o Yoo-nah Prach-o-da-yat

Group chanting of the Gayatri is very stirring. One of the author's classes at the University of New Mexico used to meet a half hour early, with rhythm instruments, and chant-sing the Gayatri into the sunset.

By ourselves it is good to place the Mantra (all four lines) in the third eye spot of the forehead, with eyes closed, and to sing it mentally. Once the mind gets used to it, and builds the habit energy (Vashana) of the Gayatri, the practicer will begin to experience deep meditation with all its rest and joy.

Those who chant the Gayatri regularly appear to throw off worries and begin to act joyously. It seems to be good therapy. Often we find ourselves chanting it — orally or mentally — in time to our footsteps while walking. The

Gayatri, perhaps irrationally, seems to offer us joy, and habitual joy is healing.

Just as the Sufis chant "Yahoo," many religions in Japan use the sounds from the Lotus Sutra, the "Namu Myoho Renge Kyo." Nichiren Buddhism pioneered this chanting in Japan (the modern-day Soka Gakai religion is derived from the Nichiren). Helped by the power of its chanting which, with belief in the mystic Mandala, or Gohonzen, fulfills all desires, Nichiren has become one of the fastest growing faiths in the United States and in the world.

Much has been said in this book about the "Amida Buddha" sect of Japanese Buddhism. It is very touching to watch whole families chanting the Nembutsu, "Namu Amida Butsu," in unison, and the faces show the intense devotion that springs from it. There are many Shin Buddhist churches in the United States, so Americans who are attracted by this simple but profound practice will easily find others with whom to chant.

CONCLUSION

There are innumerable chants and many ways to utter them. One who chants regularly with a group will tend to lose his self-consciousness, and selflessness is the beginning of health. Religious chanting is a robust practice and easy to do. The author has often heard the touching chanting at Tenrikyo morning and evening services in Japan, while the adherants do the simple "dance" movements that have much in common with Moving Meditation. Tenrikyo promises its women "painless childbirth," so perhaps there is great strength in their chanting.

One of the weaknesses of the Japanese Healing Church (Sekai Kyu Seikyo) is the fact that they use Christian hymns and Shinto chants; they have not yet developed their own focus. However, the Shinto prayer they chant, the "Taka Amahara," has great power. One can find this church under the name "Church of World Messianity" in Los Angeles and, whether one goes there for the healing power of the "Johrei" practice or to chant the "Taka Amahara" with others, he will find strong healing vibrations.

Chanting is about the easiest of all meditative practices. In the beginning it is not actually true meditation, but when one closes his eyes mentally, it becomes deep and profound meditation. With many this chanting goes on in their hearts all the time. Meaningful chanting is great therapy.

Chapter 11
MIND CONTROL — ZEN
Instruction and Commentary

Everything that happens in Zen is meditation in its true sense. One not only does Zazen (Zen "sitting in meditation") at formal meditation times, with his mind properly controlled he is also doing Zazen while washing his teeth or plowing the field.

The word "Zen" literally means "meditation." It is the Japanese pronunciation of the written character for the Chinese "Ch'anna," and Ch'anna is as close as the Chinese can come to pronouncing "Jhanna," the word for meditation in the Indian Pali language. So Zen is the meditation sect of Buddhism, whereas other sects rely on philosophy, study of the scriptures, remembrance of the name of Buddha, and even proper conduct for their principle practice.

"Things are as they are," say the Zen Masters. Generally, we do not see them that way. In our everyday lives our emotions color our responses and bring needless fear and tension — with resulting ill-health. We hear a high-pitched sound and distinguish it as a siren, then translate it into some form of disaster. Eating, we are worrying about the morrow and miss the enjoyment of the food. Zen says the emotion and reason must be brought into balance, or there will be suffering. Zen wants us to see and hear and feel things as they are *NOW* without coloring the facts or over-reacting. A story may illustrate this point:

Takusan, the Chinese Zen master, came upon one of his best disciples doing intense Zazen in the meditation hall. The master cocked one eye at his earnest student. Looking up, the disciple shook his head despairingly. "A dark night and no travelers," he commented, obviously discouraged. "Master, I am cold!" he complained piteously.

Instead of commiserating, Takusan swung into action. Whirling quickly, he cracked first one, then the other hand across the sitting disciple's face. The blows were unexpected, and they hurt. The disciple jumped to his feet and, as the master closed in to rain more blows on him, turned and ran down the corridor. Out of the meditation hall they went, master furiously chasing pupil. Down one path and up another they flew until, finally, the disciple, panting and perspiring, was cornered at a dead-end spot in the garden. He turned to face his attacker.

"Are you warm now?" snarled the master. A light dawned on the disciple; he was warm all right!

This is real teaching, though we may have a difficult time realizing it. The Zen way of thinking is not the usual chain of dualistic concepts. In his book *Zen Meditation [A Broad View]* the author expounds this point at some length, pointing out that we ordinarily think in "either/or" terms, whereas Zen's way of thinking could be characterized as "neither/nor." Quite logically we feel that, if it is not big, it must be small. If you don't agree with me, you disagree. But Zen is not limited by these boundaries. A surveyor may see only one area of the mountain, but Zen wants us to take in the entire mountain at one time. This is real meditation. We are not limited by "yea" and not by "nay"; all things are right in their way. An illustration:

The Chinese Zen Master, Takusan, was walking thru his monastery with a young attendant. In the corridor he came upon two monks arguing bitterly, and he paused, waiting for an explanation.

The first monk began: "Yesterday you told us to do so-and-so, and I was doing as you instructed. This fellow misunderstands and I am trying to explain it to him. Am I wrong?"

Takusan shook his head. "You are right," was his pronouncement, much to the dismay of the other monk, who immediately began to offer his version of the misunderstanding.

"You are right," agreed Takusan, nodding his head in the direction of the second monk.

The young attendant was floored by this unexpected turn. "They can't *both* be right!" he protested.

Again Takusan nodded. "And I perceive that you, too, are right," he conceded.

This is a good example of a higher type of thinking in operation, not bound by the narrow "either/or," so habitual with us. Zen training, and Zen meditation, jolt us out of our comfortable way of looking at things. Why do we put up with this nonsense and forego our ease? Nobody forces us to do so.

Strangely enough, those who undergo the strict discipline of Zen usually report greater peace of mind, improvement in health, and the onset of an irrational cheerfulness. Seemingly without enough sleep, sitting long hours with painful crossed legs, and occasionally stimulated by the threat of the master's big stick, Zen practicers tell of losing their neuroses and casting off their allergies. Strange! Why does one leave the "good life," and luxuries and diversions available to the well-to-do, and seclude himself on a mountain top, arising at 3:30 a.m. in the freezing snow, to undergo the tortures of facing himself in the long meditation sittings? There must be an answer. Perhaps a fear of death, horror at the thought of all this impermanence, and thirst for ultimate answers may somewhat explain the puzzling conduct. Just let there be some success in the practice and a great, unshakable joy comes over the aspirant. Let him experience even a mild Satori and he cries with bliss — his life is permanently changed. As the author's friend, Zen writer Paul Reps, says: "It doesn't make sense; it makes you!" Saint John of the Cross counseled: to have everything, we simply have to want nothing. Whatever one's religious leanings, a taste of Zen will deepen them and contribute to one's overall well-being.

INSTRUCTION (Part One)

In theory, it is best to sit in full Lotus position, with each foot turned up on the opposite thigh. Although we sit on a slightly raised pillow in Zazen, this position, and even the half-Lotus (where one foot is turned up on the opposite thigh) are actually too difficult for most modern-day students; they generally sit in a cross-legged position with one leg flat on the floor and the other flat on top of it (see illustration, figure A).

Eyes are kept slightly open, gazing down at the mat a few feet in front, and the head is set back on the shoulders (like a cadet's) and just slightly lowered. The back, of course, is held straight and, in Japanese Zen, the lower chest is thrust out (the Chinese sit in a more relaxed pose). In Japan today the right hand is wrapped around the back of the left and the two thumbs meet in an extended arc, the base of the hands being pushed in against the belly (see figure B).*

---

*Note: The two illustrations are from *Zen Meditation* [*A Broad View*], by Justin Stone (Sun Publishing Co.)

Figure A

In ancient China, and even in Japan, it is believed the hand positions were with the right hand folding over the left, the right thumb digging into the left palm, and the middle finger of the left hand pressed into the palm of the right. This position makes sense, as the thumb and middle finger link up the Meridian Channels (as in acupuncture) and allow the Chi to circulate freely during the sitting. This circulation is very important as the limbs will tend to become stiff and painful when the Zen aspirant first begins sitting. In the old days, when the pain in the knees was severe, a sitter might place one palm under the knee and one over it, or one under the sole of the foot and one on top of the knee, so as to allow the Chi to flow freely thru the offending spot and relieve the pain. The sitter sits, quietly, in full awareness, and does not move when the position becomes uncomfortable.

COMMENTARY

Although there is emphasis on formal sitting (whether in Temples, Zendoes, or at home), Zen talks most of "mind." This "mind" is not to be confused with our thinking process, however. Actually, it is a translation of the Chinese word "shin" ("kokoro" in Japanese), which can mean heart, mind, or spirit, with some overtones of consciousness. When other Buddhist philosophies speak of "mind only," it is close to what we think of as "nothing but spirit." However, Zen warns us against indulging in conceptions, and rigid phrases do build conceptual images. Zen is interested in the practicer having the Zen experience, not in talking about it. "Only the taster knows if the water is hot or cold," advises the Zen teacher. Zen implores us to know this "mind"; in fact, we are told to confront it face to face! This is what is meant when Zen demands that we show the teacher "our original face

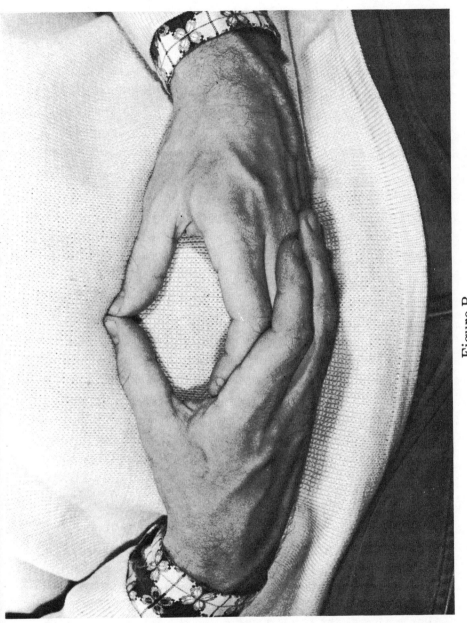

Figure B

before we were born." Until we rest in our True Nature we are fragmented and sick.

Although we must uncover ourselves, Zen strongly advises us to sit without conceptual thinking in Zazen pose. It says the greatest benefits will accrue to us if we sit quietly this way. While the consciousness will not be acting in the ordinary manner for the experienced sitter — he will be hearing sounds, seeing sights, and even having random thoughts, but not attaching to them and not reacting to them — there will be no trance state, no euphoric lassitude. Tests have shown that the pulse actually picks up during the sitting, though the experienced sitter may be as still as a dead man on the outside. Inside there is a heightened livingness; there is no other way to explain it. The meditator is in the state of the greatest attention and utmost awareness, though he is directing his awareness within instead of spending it on objects.

Zen speaks of "Sudden Enlightenment." This does not mean no training is needed! The experience itself does not come by degrees; it flashes like lightning and one is re-made. Driving from Los Angeles to the beautiful village of Carmel, California, one travels over three hundred miles, then comes to the top of a hill and suddenly sees the town set down against the ocean. It is an abrupt seeing after traveling three hundred miles.

The author's Zen teacher spoke of two types of Satori experience, the first an overwhelming sense of Unity in which the feeling of Oneness erases all the differentiation in life, and the second in which one is able to observe his own Satori. The second is necessary so that we will not be hung up in an "other-worldly" state; if we had only the first, the mountains would no longer be mountains. But then we have the second, we make the full circle, and the mountain again becomes a mountain. Once again we can function in the world. The author has known a few who have had revealing spiritual experiences and become stuck in the awe of "Oneness." Their way is thereafter quite difficult — completely idealistic. We must live in this world, and we learn to understand ourselves thru relationships with others. If we think that because we are vegetarians and "pure" we are somehow better than non-vegetarians, we do not understand, and we are not "pure." When Chuang-Tzu spoke of the "fasting mind," he meant to drop such accretions, as they are not natural. Only thru the natural and spontaneous can we realize ourselves. We must never forget that to "fast" is to do without greed, anger, and delusion. So we must make the full circle back to humanity and all beings.

INSTRUCTION (Part Two)

The author is going to outline a little known four-part meditation taught by the Chinese LinChi ("Rinzai" in Japanese). We work on it sitting in meditation pose, or we can contemplate it sitting on a train. Strangely, though it was a creation of Rinzai's, and Rinzai Zen is dominant in Japan, this four-way meditation does not seem to be practiced in the islands of Nippon.

In the first part, we concentrate on the object only, completely eliminating the subject.

In the second part, our concentration is on the one meditating, the subject, and we eliminate any object.

In the third part, we concentrate on both the subject and the object.

Finally, we eliminate *both* the subject and the object — and just meditate.

This meditation is hard work, but not difficult to do. There are many practices of this sort in Zen, but we do not have to do them all. Rinzai's four-part way is quite enough for us.

CONCLUSION

Zen speaks a good deal of Void or Emptiness. However, until we have the experience of this "Shunyata," as it is called in all Buddhism, such words are just concepts. To intellectually grasp the Void is impossible; it is only known experientially. One teacher taught his disciple what the Void is by grasping his nose and almost twisting it off! Such "emptiness" one is not apt to forget.

Zen practice brings a clarity of mind that is the best tonic. If we completely succeed, we do the impossible, like climbing a hundred-foot pole, then taking another step! In Soto Zen it is said that the practice itself *is* the Enlightenment. We seek nothing, and, like St. John of the Cross, we then have everything.

The mind that is contented and not overcome with unfulfillable desires is healthy. The one who sees things as they are is a "realist," and yet he becomes a most spiritual figure. Self-pity melts with Zazen; gratitude takes its place. Having nothing, we are grateful for it. A light dawns: we open our eyes and there it is. It is no wonder that many psychologists have been attracted to Zen practice. Becoming whole, we are healthy. Knowing ourselves as we truly are, with all the warts and blemishes, we are healed.

Chapter 12
MOVING MEDITATION
Instruction and Commentary

Of all the meditations, it seems the ones most fitting for Westerners are the Moving Meditations. It is easier to move joyously than it is to sit quietly and attempt to control the mind. The latter effort demands a quiet place and considerable motivation on the part of the meditator. T'ai Chi Chih, the Moving Meditation, can be done by anyone anywhere. Moreover, it requires no space other than that in which one stands, no special clothing, and no semi-dark sound-free location. It seems appropriate for any age at any time except directly after meals and just before going to bed. The effects are those of meditation, as well as of an energizing exercise. The mind is stilled, and a joyous physical glow spreads over the body. The Chi flows, one feels good, and 100 chronic ailments seem to improve or disappear. This is a truly healing practice.

Before getting to the instruction part of this chapter, it might be useful to talk a bit about the origin and philosophy of the T'ai Chi disciplines. T'ai Chi Ch'uan is an ancient practice, usually a series of 108 connected movements, appearing almost like a slow dance of unusual beauty. It sometimes takes years to master this involved form, but the time spent is well worth the prolonged effort. However, older people have trouble with some of the movements, and many find they cannot memorize the long, semi-abstract routine that can take 18 or 30 minutes to perform. Usually it is a matter of years before the practicer notices the flow of the Chi to the extent that it is curative, seems to lengthen life, and brings great serenity.

"T'ai Chi Chih" is a creation of the author's, utilizing the same Yin-Yang principles as apply to T'ai Chi Ch'uan. From several ancient movements, which the author was fortunate enough to learn from an old and wise Chinese, he has created 20 movements (four adapted from T'ai Chi Ch'uan) that can be performed in any order. One does not even have to master the 20; frequent practice of six or eight will cause the Chi to flow to a great extent, and this Chi is not only Prana (intrinsic energy), it is also Prajna (wisdom, the intuitive knowing, not accumulated knowledge). It is interesting that new students of T'ai Chi Chih (courses for beginners generally encompass only seven lessons) usually feel the flow of Chi almost immediately, first in the fingers, and then, if the concentration below the navel or in the soles of the feet is maintained, thruout the system. In one set of movements the six secret Healing Sounds of Taoism are utilized. Spectators watching a class perform the movements while chanting the Healing Sounds have remarked that the energy in the room seemed ready to explode!

It is impossible to learn the longer discipline, T'ai Chi Ch'uan, from a book. A good teacher is needed, plus patience (and means) to continue the study for some time. Therefore, we will just refer to it, with admiration. (The author has taught the Yang Form of T'ai Chi Ch'uan at two universities, and performs it at least once every day.) On the other hand, it is not difficult to instruct a reader in a few of the T'ai Chi Chih movements, and we will do so in this chapter.

To discuss the philosophy behind the two T'ai Chi practices, we must refer to (1) its Cosmic significance, and (2) its effect in and on the body.

In Chinese Acupuncture it is believed that there are many Meridian channels in the body thru which the Vital Force (Chi, Prana) flow. Eight principle Meridians are referred to in Chinese medicine, closely following the findings of the Taoist sages in their spiritual practices. When the Yin Chi and Yang Chi (negative energy and positive energy) are out of balance, there is illness — and by illness is also meant the circumstances of man's life. For those dualistically oriented, it is hard to understand the relationship of the Macrocosmic (whole) with the Microcosmic (individual). However, holistic medicine is based on just such a relationship.When we note that the great Yang is the sun and, in man's body, the heart; and the great Yin is the earth, corresponding to the kidneys in the body, we begin to get the idea. Of course, Chinese philosophy — and medicine — refer to the "lead of the kidney region," thus bringing in the elements. Moreover, the time of day and season of the year play an important part, but such understanding is not necessary to our practice. Suffice to say, our goal is to freely circulate the Vital Force and bring it into balance with either T'ai Chi Ch'uan or T'ai Chi Chih. Once we know and practice one or the other, this goal is easily reached.

First a word about the Cosmology. "T'ai Chi" is usually translated as "Supreme Ultimate," being synonymous with "Tao." "Chih" means "knowing," or "knowledge" when the proper Chinese written character is used. Thus "T'ai Chi Chih" means "Knowing the Supreme Ultimate," which is the deepest purpose of the practice. In his fine book, *The Practice of Zen*, Garma C.C. Chang has a chapter on meditative ways to Enlightenment, and he refers to T'ai

Chi as a very definite path to attain Samadhi, the super-conscious state that is the final goal of Yoga. Although most people come to T'ai Chi practice for benefits in health and longevity, they often remain to receive the deeper Enlightenment boons. The author has seen those crippled by arthritis or rheumatism who, later, appeared straight and healed, but also definitely changed spiritually. One Hollander suffered from torture in the Pacific war and, after his recovery, became a T'ai Chi instructor.

The Chinese say we first have the Undefined Reality, in the "beginning" and we would delineate this as an empty circle ◯ . There is a stirring of two forces, and they come into manifestation ☯ . The black is the Yin (receptive, contracting, dark, cold, negative, female) and the white is the Yang (creative, expanding, light, heat, positive, male). Note the little bit of "male" in the "female," and vice-versa. This makes possible the shifting from too much Yin to an over balance of Yang, and also the opposite. It is said that, when one force becomes too strong, it changes into the other — extreme Yin becomes Yang, and so forth.

Note that the Yin Chi and the Yang Chi appear before there is even a universe, let alone man to inhabit it. The combination (always shifting, always bringing about change) of the two forces brings into existence Heaven (Yang), Earth (Yin), and Man, the result of the "wedding" of the two. This is expressed in Japanese flower arrangement by the triangle — heaven, man, earth.

Man combines the Yang of Heaven and Yin of Earth in various balances.

From Heaven, Earth, and Man come the "10,000 things," the world of phenomena. If we work backward, by balancing the Chi, we bring the Yin and Yang back into equilibrium and, in such way, can lead up to the undifferentiated Reality, the Supreme Ultimate. So our cirulating and balancing practice apparently bring health and longevity along the way and, ultimately, take us back to the wholeness of our being. In a sense, this is also Zen practice, realizing our True Nature (arriving at the Source).

T'ai Chi Chih Teachers Training class, Albuquerque, New Mexico, January 1976.

Figure 1

Figure 2

Figure 3

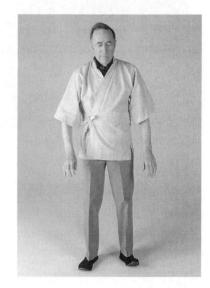

Figure 4

THE ROCKING MOTION

Figure 5

Stand in a relaxed manner, feet slightly apart. The arms are at the sides and the hands are turned so the palms face the front (see FIGURE 1).

Now slowly rock forward with the hands lifting to the front. As you rock forward, rise up on your toes (see FIGURE 2).

Turn your hands so the palms face down as you begin to lower the arms and you come down off your toes (see FIGURE 3).

As you swing down, the arms extend to the back and you naturally rock back on your heels (FIGURE 4).

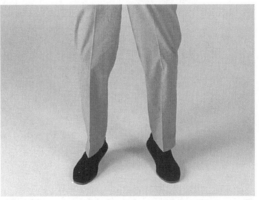

Figure 6

Turn your palms to the front (FIGURE 1) and begin your upward swing again (FIGURES 2, 3, 4).

Note: FIGURE 5 shows the position of the feet in FIGURE 2, up on the toes. FIGURE 6 shows the position of the feet in FIGURE 4, when you are back on your heels.

Comment: There is complete relaxation in the swings, but the air is felt to be very heavy. Fingers are spread slightly apart. 3-5 minutes of rocking should be sufficient.

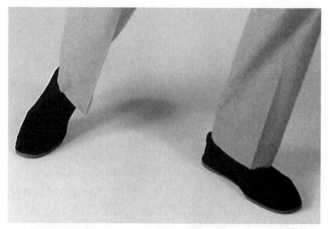

Figure 1

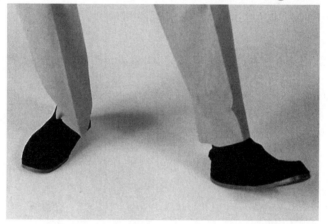

Figure 2

BASIC LEG MOVEMENTS (left side)

Put the left foot forward and slightly to the side. At FIGURE 1 you rock forward so the right heel lifts off the ground.

At FIGURE 2 you rock back so the left toe comes off the ground.

Note: It is suggested these two movements of the legs be practiced before the following T'AI CHI CHIH motions are practiced. They will be the basic leg movements for about half of the succeeding moves you will learn.

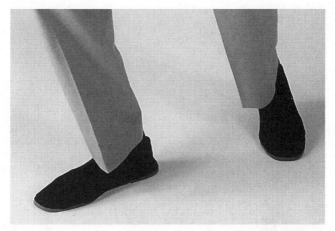

Figure 3

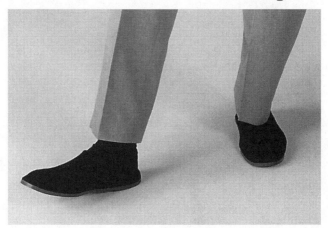

Figure 4

BASIC LEG MOVEMENTS (right side)

Here the right foot is forward and slightly to the side. At FIGURE 3 rock forward so the left heel lifts off the ground.

At FIGURE 4 rock back so the right toe comes off the ground.

Note: These foot movements, left and right, will be co-ordinated with hand movements in the pages to follow.

Figure 1

Figure 2

Figure 3

Figure 4

AROUND THE PLATTER

The left foot is placed forward in the Basic Leg Movement Position.

Elbows come close to sides, we bend the wrists, spread the fingers, and begin the movement at the chest (FIGURE 1).

Moving in a circle, from left to right, around an imaginary round platter, we shift the weight forward (FIGURE 2). As the left knee bends and the right heel comes off the ground.

At FIGURE 3 we begin to circle back on the far side of the platter, and the weight begins to shift back. At FIGURE 4 the weight has shifted back to the right leg, knee bent, and the left toes come off the ground. The hands are now back at the chest, having circled the platter.

Now repeat this movement with right foot forward and left in rear, but with the hand movement moving in a circle from right to left.

Note: Hands are relaxed, no tension. The circular movement should be made slowly, and the bending of the knees and shifting of the weight — Yinning and Yanning — is all important.

Moving Meditation

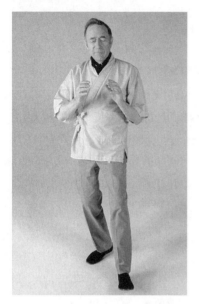

Figure 1

Figure 2

Figure 3

Figure 4

BASS DRUM

We imagine there is a small bass drum strapped to our chest, and we are going to move the hands around it in a vertical circle moving toward us.

At FIGURE 1 the weight is on the rear foot, and the toes of the left forward foot being off the ground. Hands are almost one foot apart, palms facing each other.

At FIGURE 2 the hands dip to go around the bottom of the drum and the weight begins to shift forward. At FIGURE 3 the hands are rising at the far side of the circle (drum) and the weight is on the front foot (knee bent) with the right heel off the ground.

At FIGURE 4 we have completed the circle, hands moving back toward body and weight shifting back to the position in FIGURE 1.

Now repeat this movement with right foot forward and left in rear with the same hand movement.

Note: Hands should be constantly kept the same distance apart. In Taiwan a stick somewhat like a bone is held, so the two hands must remain equidistant apart.

When one performs the movements, they should be done in a soft and relaxed manner — "softness and continuity" is the expression teachers continually use. Complete relaxation, to the point of limpness, is essential, as any tension will keep the Chi from flowing properly thru the channels.

Once the moves are mastered — which should not take long — the practicer should begin placing his concentration in the soles of the feet and keeping it there all thru practice (the spot two inches below the navel is also good, but it is more difficult to find mentally). Having the thought down below, with no extraneous thoughts, will "bring the heart-fire down," which is the basis of the healing and energizing we want. We should not allow the negative Yin of the kidneys to rise. Our thought is concentration on the spot below.

COMMENTARY

Since we are primarily dealing with the Chi (and mastery of the Chi, or Prana, is the great secret of healing), it seems appropriate to extract one paragraph from the voluminous writings of the modern-day Indian sage, Sri Aurobindo, as follows:

"There is one all-pervading life or dynamic energy (Chi, Prana), the material aspect being only its outermost movement. It creates all these forms of the physical universe. Even if the whole figure of the universe was abolished, it (Chi) would still go on existing and would be capable of creating a new universe in its place."

In the body, we feel this Cosmic Force as the Yin Chi and the Yang Chi. What is the significance of this Yin-Yang relationship? Let us quote from the age-old writings of the Chinese sage, Huang Ti:

"The principle of Yin and Yang is the basis of the entire universe. It is the principle of everything in creation. It brings about the transformation to parenthood; it is the root and source of life and death . . .

"Heaven was created by an accumulation of Yang; Earth was created by an accumulation of Yin.

"The ways of Yin and Yang are to the left and to the right. Water and Fire are the symbols of Yin and Yang and are the source of power of everything in creation.

"Yang ascends to Heaven; Yin descends to Earth. Hence the universe (Heaven and Earth) represents motion and rest, controlled by the wisdom of nature. Nature grants the power to beget and to grow, to harvest and to store, to finish and begin anew."

The above quotation harmonizes very well with the cryptic inscription the author's Zen master wrote in Chinese Calligraphy: "Old bamboo grove, new shoots." This seems to say it all.

Parenthetically, the author has often realized, thru meditation, that "time" seems to be expansion and contraction (periodic or cyclical, not caused), so "time" becomes the interplay of Yin and Yang.

It is not truly necessary that the practicer understand these practical theories, but knowing a little of the background may motivate him to do the simple practice and receive the many benefits. For one, he may note an increased flow of sexual energy, which he can use as he wishes. Often impotence seems to yield to the stimulus of the flow, with the resulting benefit to marriages. Many also note an increase of patience, a feeling of well-being that takes away all urgency. Indeed, many varieties of benefits have been described in letters to the author. Perhaps it might be relevant to share excerpts from a few of many letters so that the reader, seeking healing effects, can determine if his particular problems have been dealt with by others.

Letter from J.B. (male, who has since become a T'ai Chi Chih instructor):

"Rapic weight loss was the first and most obvious physical change. I have lost 65 pounds and am still losing slowly, although I appear to be stabilizing at an optimum weight. Last Wednesday, after swimming a mile, my pulse was 105 and respiration only slightly elevated. Endurance on the tennis and handball courts has improved greatly. The amazing fact concerning my weight loss is that at no time have I attempted to control my diet. In fact, I now eat more than I did when I was 65 pounds heavier. It appears that my metabolism has changed completely." (J.B.'s wife also reports a weight loss of almost 25 pounds.)

"My blood pressure under stress conditions has dropped from approximately 140/95 in September, 1975, to 120/75 at present." It should be noted that J.B., who had always had a weight problem, was 255 pounds when the author first knew him.

Letter from B.H. (a rather heavy girl who apparently suffered from asthma, and has since lost weight and become an accredited T'ai Chi Chih instructor):

"Before I started T'ai Chi Chih, I was taking medication for asthma and averaging trouble with asthma on the minimum of every other week and having to be on watch every place I went.

"Now since I have been doing T'ai Chi Chih for two months, I have had minimal trouble and no longer have to take medication! Or watch the places I go."

A similar letter comes from "Marian," a student who lives on the Monterey Peninsula in California. Apparently an "incurable" heart condition cleared, to the amazement of her doctor (who thought there was something wrong with his machine when he first noted the change). It would be possible to print many, many letters, but the idea is not to cast accolades at T'ai Chi Chih practice. Rather, the author hopes such isolated examples will encourage the reader to try the beneficial discipline for himself.

There is no way one can promise that a practicer, regularly doing many or all of the 20 movements of T'ai Chi Chih, will derive similar benefits, but this is a book on healing thru meditation, and these are the results reported from practice of one of the Moving Meditations.

Is it best to study with a T'ai Chi teacher? With T'ai Chi Ch'uan it is absolutely necessary; with T'ai Chi Chih it makes an easy task even easier. However, there are those who have learned the latter discipline from the book, the result of living in an area where there are not yet any teachers.

If the reader will do the very simple T'ai Chi Chih movements taught in this chapter, for perhaps 15 or 20 minutes of repetitive practice, he should note a tingling "filling feeling" in his fingers and hands. The feeling will differ with each movement. This is the flow of the Yin Chi and Yang Chi, which separate when one is in motion. For this reason, as we end the repetition (9, 18, 36, or 72 times) of each form, we hold the hands parallel to the ground, fingers outstretched, so the Yin and Yang energy can flow back together again. Such integration is important; we do not wish to remain fragmented.

The author knows no more healing practice than this meditation, based on his own experience. He is grateful to know it, grateful that he was the channel thru which it could originate (of ourselves we create nothing), and hopes that great multitudes of people will practice the Moving Meditations to bring peace and radiant health to themselves.

Chapter 13
THE SPIRITUAL
SIDE OF MEDITATION

In order to fully appreciate the healing power of meditation, it is important that we understand the spiritual side as well as the physical and mental. Actually, the psyche is one; these three cannot be separated.

Such great leaders of mankind as Gautama Buddha, founder of a religion which has lasted 2500 years and embraces a billion people, have reached their great enlightenment thru meditation. The Buddha's aim was to do away with suffering. Is there anything more healing than to understand the causes of suffering and to be free of them? This is healing in its truest sense.

It is said that the great Yogis who have reached the Liberated State are almost impervious to ordinary illness. A sick Yogi is not a true Yogi. In truth, the spiritually advanced have dropped most of the burden that causes illness. The Buddha counseled that "true fasting" was not abstaining from eating but, doing without greed, anger, and delusion. When the hold of these three is broken, what is there to cause illness, except old karmic debts (reaction to long-past actions)?

Ultimately, all illness has spiritual roots; it is grounded in such things as delusion (mistaking the unreal for the real) and nurtured by such things as greed, anger, and resentment. The enlightened man's mind has reached the state of equanimity beyond the debilitating effects of such emotion. The Japanese Healing Church realizes these spiritual seeds that have physical manifestation, and so gets good results. All true "healers" have done the same.

However, in the long run self-healing is the only lasting healing. We change inside, and the world appears to change around us. We are no longer caught in the violent ebb and flow of the emotions, and we begin to see things as they really are, not thru the screens of affective emotion. When the mind is really still, creative and receptive, the joy of being shines thru. "To the mind that is still, the universe surrenders," says the poet. Then we are truly healed.

The spiritual task is an inner one, but the results must show outwardly in our relations to others. If we are at peace inside, we can show love to all beings. When there is turbulence, it spills over to our relationships. We cannot be half-loving and half-hating at the same time.

One of the most puzzling curiosities of our culture is the amount of self-pity in which seemingly well-fed and prosperous people indulge. This is crippling. The author has his students supplant this self-pity with gratitude; the two cannot exist in the same breast. We are not grateful for what we have — which is not lasting and so is not ours — we are grateful for what we are. When self-pity is displaced by gratitude, automatically half our illness is gone. The author made a trip thru much of Japan, staying at the simple Tenrikyo Church centers, and noticed the joy with which these people do every task. Their's is a hard life, living without running hot water and other modern conveniences, and yet there is a joy pervading life in those centers. The answer seems to lie in their slogan: "Joyous Life!" They do not mean that you should *try* to be joyous;

they say it is your *duty* to be joyous, you have no business spreading negative vibrations. This "Arigatai" (gratefulness), with not too many things to be grateful for, is the secret of their joy. These are healthy people, and we can learn much from them.

By doing some of the meditations in this book, one will begin to get insights into impermanence, and the struggle against the lack of the permanent is one of the great causes of unhappiness, worry, and, ultimately, illness. I have a wonderful job, a beautiful young wife, and two lovely children. We live in a fine old home in a pleasant neighborhood. So I assume I will *always* have these beneficial possessions in their present state. Although I dimly realize there are accidents, people lose jobs, houses can be destroyed by fire, and children go astray, I am certain none of these mishaps could ever happen to me. My status is a permanent one; my wife will always be beautiful.

But is life like that? The Chinese say: "The wise man goes to his triumph like a funeral." He does not rejoice in his brief moment of good fortune; well does he know that too much Yang (positive) can quickly turn into Yin (negative). In our world, every day we see people destroyed, not by impermanence, but by their failure to understand and accept impermanence. In 1929, when the stock market crashed and people's fortunes were quickly dissolved, the answer for many was immediate suicide! This is incredible. It is the result of the failure to comprehend the inevitability of change. "The only thing permanent is change itself," says the wise *Book of Changes*, the ancient Chinese *I Ching*.

When, thru meditaion, we come to realize that joy comes from within and has nothing to do with objects, neither possessions nor lack of possessions, we are already free of the demon of necessity. "I have to have that!" means frustration, sooner or later.

When a strong desire is gratified, it is not the acquisition that gives us a short-lived feeling of elation; it is the great emptiness we feel once we are relieved of the apprehension of that desire that makes us joyous — until, once again, the heart runs after something burdensome and we feel, once more, an incompleteness. When St. John of the Cross said we can have everything if only we want nothing, he was expressing a paradox from which we can learn a great lesson. The "fasting mind" does not push us to ceaselessly acquire; it counsels us to cut down on the acquisitive taste. Two cars, a swimming pool, and three television sets hardly equate equanimity to the possessor.

One time an enlightened friend was having dinner with the author. As we were about to bite into the delicious Sachar torts that came for dessert, she suddenly asked: "Can we do without these?" In answer we both pushed the appealing pastries aside.

"Okay, we might as well eat them!" was her verdict, graphically illustrating that we can only enjoy what we can do without.

Those who practice holistic medicine well know illness, particularly chronic complaints, cannot be cured thru drugs that drive down the fever or act as a palliative to the apparent symptom. "There's a bug going around," hardly serves as an explanation for the ills that mankind suffers, or the growing amount of mental illness that crowds our hospitals. Something deeper is needed. Ignoring symptoms (except as indicators), the ancient Chinese attempted to determine if the life force, the Chi, itself was out of balance, too positive or too negative. When this vital force was back in balance, the symptoms dropped by the wayside. The author, in the chapter on Moving Meditation, has shown has such a spiritual exercise as T'ai Chi Chih seems to bring the Yang and the Yin together and reintegrate the individual — with the results mentioned in the delighted letters received, having to do with weight control, asthma, eye trouble, high blood pressure, etc. These are very real manifestations and they seem to respond to the true spiritual disciplines practiced in the various forms of meditation.

Whether one believes or one does not believe, the sincere practice of meditation should bring results. With the life in greater harmony, the ills tend to disappear. And, as the ailments leave, a joy is uncovered and we find we get lasting (spiritual) benefits far beyond what we had anticipated from our meditative practice.

Chapter 14
SUMMING UP

The purposes of this book are basically three: (1) to show how true meditation heals our ills (2) to offer instruction in various types of meditation, indicating their probable effects, and (3) to offer a glimpse of what the future of the "healing arts" might be.

"True meditation" is a term we use because sitting and day-dreaming, wandering around in idle thought, is not really meditation. Concentration and a focused mind are implied in meditation, of whatever nature. An experienced meditator is as purposeful as a carpenter. He has a task and the necessary tools to accomplish it, so he goes right to work. It is best that the meditator have this determined attitude, though he must not consciously try for results in meditation. The attitude-of-no-attitude is best. Meditation should always be kept posititve, for reasons mentioned in the section on "Danger in Meditation" in the appendix.

Instruction in many types of meditation is necessary because most would-be meditators — and doctors recommending the practice — are not aware there are many modes of meditation, each causing a different effect. This point has been well stressed in the book. All meditations offer healing possibilities, but some encourage awareness of the "Now," while others bring about an "other-worldly" attitude. Still others directly stimulate the flow of the Chi and development of an inner heat which is particularly effective in self-healing. Mere wishful thinking or a positive attitude will avail nothing; the meditator should choose the proper tools and use them correctly, hence the detailed instructions.

This matter of the inner heat and the radically changed vibration has to do with point number three, the future of the healing arts. The author confidently believes that, one day, the sick person will be shown how to quickly arouse a great inner heat, a healing vibration that will have almost instant effect. The Nei Kung and T'ai Chi Chih are two meditations that work toward that end, and the author has observed surprising, sometimes hard to believe, results from these meditations. For instance, the amazing weight loss of J.B. (reported in the chapter on Moving Meditation) was not the result of perspiration and violent effort; it was the circulating effect of the Chi, causing internal heat, which burned up the calories so quickly. Those who do T'ai Chi Chih — and, to a lesser degree, those who do other meditations — know how thirsty they become during practice. This is due to the circulation of the vital force and is reported in all the classic T'ai Chi Ch'uan texts, where it is said that the flowing Chi "burns up the acqueous excess." It must be stressed that J.B.'s closest friend, who was six feet one inch tall and weighed 155 pounds, actually *gained* ten pounds on the same diet during the same period of time. The key here is the phrase "acqueous *excess.*" The changing of the metabolism that J.B. refers to carries with it a great deal of wisdom; those underweight do not seem to lose.

There are those who hope one day there will be booths where a pushed button will raise vibration and cure most ills. The author is not that sanguine; he believes it is an inner task, demanding the effort of meditation and perseverance of practice. It is hoped that those believing in holistic medicine will study the examples given in this book with an open mind. The possibilities are here.

Particularly in the chapter on "Raising the Dumo Heat" are indications of what might be possible. Effects from such a radical change in body temperature can be almost instantaneous, the author believes. It should certainly, with such inner methods, be possible for man to achieve a much longer life span, perhaps equal to his great potential. In India (and among the American Indians) it is believed that, in past ages, man was much bigger than now and had a far greater life expectancy. Some ancient Eastern statues attest to that belief. All that is needed is an open mind and the willingness to practice. Man has much greater powers than he knows.

Many students and friends have come to the author for "spiritual counceling." He tends to turn them away. What is usually wanted is a quick cure, a pill for loneliness, poverty, or general melancholy. If the visitor will take steps himself (such as practice of meditation or T'ai Chi), the loneliness and poverty may disappear of themselves. After all, being poor is a comparative matter; it's all in how one sees it. One woman was very bitter because she and her husband had to share a bathroom, and all their richer friends had separate bathrooms. This is hardly poverty, but it was enough to bring very real suffering to her.

The one suffering loneliness becomes gloomy, and this attitude drives others away, and so there is loneliness! If, instead of being caught in this bitter circle, a turn 180 degrees to the inside is made and an uncovering of the joy that is natural to our being is effected, the gloom will be dissolved. Practice, not sermons or pills, will correct the situation. The quality of the Chi flowing thru us must change, and we are already aware of the explanation (in the early part of the book) of the reciprocal character of Mind and Chi. When the Chi changes, the state of mind is altered. This is the great secret and the basis of real healing. It is said that, at the moment of enlightenment for the Zen adept, there is a complete "revulsion" of the Chi. The whole personality may change and one is remade. To heal, we change what is inside, what flows thru us and makes us what we are. As the state of mind changes, the Chi changes — and vice-versa. Here is the key to healing. "When the body is mastered, the mind is mastered," counseled the Buddha, further instructing that the opposite is also true.

When, finally, man comes to an understanding of the Meditative Way, and follows it, he will understand the sublime message of hope given in the scripture known as the "Lotus Sutra":

"From the state of emptiness, each man's body is a body pervading the universe, his voice is a voice filling the universe, his life is a life which is without limit."

APPENDIX

Lotus symbol used in Shingon Meditation.

MEDITATION HEALING CHART

RELIEF FROM STRESS	Japa Breath-Dhyana	Complete rest due to immersion in non-ego Trance-state
ENERGIZING	Reverse Meditative Breathing Nei Kung Moving Meditations	Directly stimulates the intrinsic energy (Chi)
SUDDEN INSIGHT	Chi K'uan Zen (Zazen)	Mental discipline Understanding of impermanence, relief from fear Satori may result
QUICK PHYSICAL HEALING	Tibetan Dumo Heat Reverse Meditative Breathing Moving Meditations Nei Kung	Visualization, actively circulating healing energy
PSYCHOLOGICAL INSIGHT	Satipatthana	Self-analysis, 24-hour mindfulness
WEIGHT CONTROL — SERENITY	Moving Meditations (T'ai Chi Chih, T'ai Chi Ch'uan)	Centering, balancing internal energy
DEVOTIONAL	Chanting (Nembutsu, Lotus Sutra, Gayatri, Heart Sutra)	Countering self-pity with gratitude

DANGERS IN MEDITATION

Many meditations can *be sexually stimulating, arousing the Kundalini force and causing the Chi [intrinsic energy] to flow dramatically. Particularly in Chinese and Japanese meditation, we bring the flow of force to the center two inches below the navel, which is extremely close to the sexual zone.*

Antidote: Do the reverse meditative breathings (particularly the first part known as "The Great Circle Meditation"). This will transmute the sex energy into a higher form of energy, if that is what is desired.

If meditation becomes too passive [as in self-hypnosis or candle-gazing], there is real danger of obsession or possession from outside.

Antidote: Use the Mantra, breath-counting, or any other technique very positively. Even if meditative trance can be achieved without technique, such meditation can easily become passive, so the Mantra or specified formula *should* be used.

Meditation in rooms with bad air, or in soft, reclining comfortable chairs can be harmful.

Antidote: The back should be straight in meditation so the force can travel easily thru the internal channels. Relaxation in reclining soft chairs should be avoided; not only may it cause the meditator to fall asleep, but the circulation is not good. Always sit in a upright chair or in cross-legged meditative pose on the floor or mat. The pranic content being all-important, and associated with the air breathed, meditation in over-heated air or in foul atmosphere can be definitely harmful. Cold is not harmful, and good meditation will warm the meditator, so put on another sweater, do some T'ai Chi first, or do breathing exercises, but do the meditative practice in fresh air!

Some beginning meditators begin to do "Astral Traveling." They are shocked to find themselves out of the body, then delighted by the tricks this allows them to play on friends. Such practice should be avoided; there is the possibility of being unable to return to the body, and the body is in a vulnerable position when the consciousness is away from it.
Antidote: Ignore such manifestations and continue with the positive meditative technique. Stay away from all practices that take you out of the body; follow faithfully your own meditation. Keep your meditation positive, keep your posture good in meditation, and always meditate in good air amid peaceful surroundings. Do not meditate in rooms where a log fire or pot-bellied stove has dried up the oxygen.

Many meditators have visions, particularly when first beginning practice. There is nothing unusual about seeing your own face in profile, or noticing trees and highways below as though you were flying over them. These signs will disappear as one gets more deeply into his meditation.

There are so-called teachers who describe such visions to their students, even writing poems about them or painting pictures. Ultimately, these visions are the products of mind. Continued visions are the sign of a disturbed mind, not of an advanced adept.

Antidote: The experienced meditator, knowing these are the products of mind (no matter how pleasing they may be) will go past them, not hang on to them or publicize them, except to his teacher, if he has one. Ignore visions, even of holy figures; in extreme cases mental delusion and even mental illness can result. If there are nightmares or such, repeat a Sutra, a Scripture, or a Mantra, and they should go away. The activities of mind can easily be understood from such visions, so they can be instructive, but do not get "hung up" on them. Continue your basic meditation quite positively, and these "makyo" (as they are called in Zen) will disappear. Meditation should end delusion, not create it. The advanced meditator will reach a state of one-pointedness in which there may be only white light at the beginning, then a "blue mass" (prana) or some such focus; he will not continue to see glamourous visions.

EPILOGUE

Throughout the world there is an evolution in consciousness beginning to manifest in many areas of life. There are many aspects of this evolution actualizing everywhere: the increasing interest in spiritual and liberational pathways, the movement towards a harmonious ecology, planet wide organizations which transcend narrow national and hemispheric limitations — to name a few of the cornerstones. Foremost amongst the many facets of this consciousness evolution is the growing Holistic Health movement which has many of its main roots and branches in America.

What are the essential elements of Holistic Health and Medicine? The following list addresses this important question:

1. Each person is his or her own best healing source. The ultimate responsibility for feeling good and being well cannot depend on another person. If a practice, system, particular healer or physician makes one *depend* upon that system or person, then holistic medicine is not being fully achieved. The old model of the health practitioner doing something *to* a person results in dependence on the outside person. More and more in holism there is a trend toward

the healing practitioner being a teacher or guide helping a person develop inner awareness and outer abilities.

2. While it will always remain necessary to have curative practices, techniques and systems, the emphasis in holism is on prevention rather than cure. In this way a person can become accustomed to concentrating on being well rather than removing sickness. This concentration itself and all the processes necessary to develop this concentration are powerful healing forces.

3. One will want to learn to look at symptoms as friends to be appreciated and understood rather than as enemies to be disliked and thereby destroyed. In this way, symptoms, which are the effect of an imbalance or dis-ease, will become the true signals they are — ready to help one focus attention on the source of the symptom, rather than on the symptoms themselves.

4. It is a trap to become enmeshed in an overly emotional reaction to what are usually conceived of as various dis-ease states. Just as symptoms can be viewed as signals, so-called dis-ease states can be viewed as potential correctional purifications. Often in progressing from a relatively unhealthy to a relatively healthy state of being, a transition period forms the bridge. During this period, if one takes a narrow view, this state can be experienced as negative. If one takes a larger view, it can be seen that one is in a state of adjustment to a new way of being. The only difference here, then, is in point of view.

5. As one takes a more encompassing view of the presence or absence of health or well-being, one begins to realize that all events inter-relate. Amount and quality of physical stimulation and practice correlates with emotional states, which correlate with communications coming in and going out, which correlate with mental processes, which correlate with relationships to other people, etc. One

begins to become aware of the wholeness of one's entire sphere of activity.

6. The broadening experience of appreciating and attending to the entire sphere of life's activity deepens the awareness of the unity underlying all parts of being, physical, mental, and spiritual. Connections are noticed everywhere. Unity rather than separateness becomes the background to all experience. This is a great healing force in itself and leads to behavior which in turn brings healing energies into one's entire circle of existence.

7. Various treatment modalities should help to increase the state of well-ness and neither directly nor indirectly make matters worse than they were before instituting the treatment regimen.

8. Diet is a central part of any holistic system. But in using the word diet, the emphasis is not necessarily on the gross food level. In this context, diet is defined as anything that comes into a person whether it is food, thought, a particular person and his or her concepts, atmosphere, habit, etc. If all that comes in is seen as material for scrutiny and attention, then a person begins to order life in such a way as to decide which elements will be influential. This practice begins with being attentive and eventually helps to develop the pure attention space which, again, is a powerful healing energy itself.

9. The underlying basis for being healthy and well and all the abilities, processes, and energies developed in becoming so, relate to the primary emergent reality of holism, Self-Realization. Throughout the entire process of learning to be well and healthy, one begins to encounter the awakening experience of experiencing the experiencer. This not only leads to an ever sharpening ability to focus on one's place in the world, but also to harmonize this entire process with each and every moment of one's existence.

In *Meditation for Healing,* Justin Stone repeatedly incorporates all of the essential elements of holistic health and medicine mentioned above. In sharing these various meditative healing practices, the entire work emerges as a readable whole, engrossing and inspiring. But with the aid of the clear and succinct meditation healing chart, one can refer to a particular health goal and its corresponding practice, concentrate on this chapter or chapters alone, and still gain much of the sense of overall unity involved in the entire work. This chart represents a summary of many helpful suggestions throughout the book as to how all people, including different health practitioners, can make the best use of which practices. The application of Zen and Satipatthana practices to the broad range of psychological inquiry from sudden recognition to ongoing insight, is a valuable connection for all psychotherapists. The great, consuming, and unifying aspects of Tibetan Dumo Heat practices are beautifully and personally described. This chapter is inspirational and challenging, displaying the need for perseverance, pure motivation, and intelligent reflection when engaging in powerful practices. The power and scope of this practice can be appreciated by noting a comment about Dumo Heat by Lama Govinda:

The image of the flame is however, as we must emphasize again, not merely a metaphor, but the expression of real experiences and of psycho-physical processes, in which all properties of fire, in their elementary [tejas] as well as in their subtle effects [taijasa] can make their appearance; warmth, heat, incandescence, purification and consumation by fire, fusion, upsurging flames, radiation, penetration, enlightenment, transfiguration, and so on.*

---

*Govinda, Lama Anagorika *Foundations of Tibetan Mysticism,* first published by Rider & Co. 1960. This American edition — 1969, seventh edition — 1975, Samuel Weiser, Inc. N.Y., N.Y. p. 165.

Epilogue

Another particularly useful and brief section of this work is the section on Dangers in Meditation and the helpful corrective antidotes.

There is a broad scope to this work without voluminous over-descriptions. Philosophy and instruction of a wide range of meditative healing practices including mental, devotional, energizing, and movement techniques, all written in a warm and personal way from Justin's depth of practice, experience, and ability, combine to give the aura of fullness and completion from which one can continue for many years to derive healing energy.

Harold A. Cohen, M.D.

GLOSSARY

ACUPUNCTURE — Traditional Chinese Yin-Yang medicine, utilizing needles, massage, and moxery (heat carried from outer skin to inner organs).

AEON — The longest possible period of time. In India, a "Kalpa" is thought of as an aeon, and it is almost unbelievably long.

AGNI — The god, or essence, of fire in Indian belief.

AKASHA — Sanskrit word for "space." Indian philosophy says that, ultimately, there are only two things in the universe, Prana (intrinsic energy) and space.

AMIDA — Japanese name for the Buddha of Infinite Light, who will take those who remember his name at least ten times to the Pure Land, the Western Paradise.

AMITABHA — Name of the Buddha of Infinite Light in India and China. Sometimes referred to as "Amitayus."

APANNA — The "negative Prana," supposedly coming up from the anus.

ARIGATAI — "Thankful" in Japanese, sometimes used as "Thankfulness."

ASHRAM — Originally a forest community gathered about

a great teacher, in India. Now used in the sense of a commune with "spiritual" intentions.

ASTRAL TRAVELING — In India they speak of the "sheaths," that is, more than one body. Aside from the gross body of flesh and blood, which is lost at death, there are other bodies which are maintained after death (and in sleep). The astral is one. Some people, deliberately or inadvertantly, have the ability to leave the physical body and travel in the astral, seeing others and other places, but invisible themselves. This is a highly dangerous practice.

AURA — It is said that there is a shimmering field of light around the body, and psychics claim they can tell the emotions of one they are watching by noting the color, depth, and intensity of this "aura." Often in religious pictures we see such a circle of light around the head of a saint. It is believed that certain types of very modern photography can photograph the aura.

SRI AUROBINDO — (first word pronounced "Shree," a term of respect) Aurobindo was educated in the British Isles and did not learn native Indian tongues until he later returned to India. He taught at the University of Baroda and was closely connected with Gandi's Independence Movement, being frequently jailed for periods of time. He is known for his "Integral Yoga," his great poem about the divinity of the sun, "Savitri," and the ashram he formed at Pondicherry, probably the largest in India.

AVATAR — A direct incarnation of the Lord. It is believed there have been ten Avatars (incarnations on earth) of Lord Vishnu, the Sustainer in the Indian trio of gods (Brahma the Creator, Vishnu the Sustainer, and Shiva the Destroyer). Krishna was a famous Avatar in India, and some believe the present-day Sai Baba is one.

AYUVERDIC — The name given to ancient traditional Indian medicine, which used such things as herbs, gems, and Mantras for healing. It is closely connected with Indian scriptures.

BACKWARD FLOWING METHOD — Known in Tibet, where it is practiced in the Left-Hand Tantra (sometimes referred to as the "Yoga of Sex"), and also by Chinese Taoists, this method consists of taking the "essence," in the form of the semen or sexual energy, back up the spine to the top of the head, transmuting the sexual energy into something higher rather than expelling it thru the sex organ. Probably the Kaballah was aware of this practice, too.

BHAGAVAN — "Lord" in the Indian languages.

BHAKTI — The practice of devotion to an aspect of the Lord. "Bhakti Yoga" is one of the major types of Yoga practice. "Japa" is essentially devotional Bhakti.

BHUH BHUVAH SVAH — The first line of the sacred Gayatri Mantra is "Om Bhuh Bhuvah Svah," with the latter three words representing earth, sky, heaven, supposedly sounds of creation ("In the beginning was the Word . . .")

BINDU — Literally means "point," an unextended point that represents the essence of life. In practice, it sometimes refers to the semen.

BODHIGAYA — A place in northeast India, not too far from Benares. It is here that Gautama sat under the Bodhi tree until he achieved perfect enlightenment at the moment of seeing the morning star; therefore, it is a sacred place of Buddhists, as the Buddha (Gautama) realized his perfection there.

BODHISATTVA — Literally, "the essence of wisdom being." A Bodhisattva is a saint on his way to becoming a

Buddha, but he takes a vow to save all sentient beings before he achieves perfection (Nirvana).

BRAHMA — The creator god of the Indian trilogy, Brahma, Vishnu, and Shiva.

BREATH-DHYANA — A name the author has given to the practice of counting either the outbreaths or inbreaths, with eyes closed, as taught by the Buddha. It leads to deep meditation, as signified by the Sanskrit word "Dhyana."

BUBBLING SPRING — In Chinese, called the "Hsueh," the important spot on the soles of the feet. This is a key acupuncture point, and it is the focus of concentration in T'ai Chi Chih.

BUDDHA — The term "Buddha" means the "Perfect One" and, with all the great sages of history that India has known, it is only applied to one person, Gautama of the Sakya nation, sometimes known as "Sakyamuni." The great Buddhist religion derives from this term applied to the founder 2500 years ago. Other Buddhas spoken of are not historical persons.

CHAKRA — Literally means "wheel." The Indians refer to four or five psychic centers in the body as chakras.

CH'ANNA or CH'AN — The Chinese name for Zen Buddhism. Literally it means "meditation," as it is a transliteration of the Pali language "Jhanna."

CHI — The intrinsic energy or vital force, synonymous with the Indian Prana. Sometimes associated with the breath, but it is actually what is doing the breathing.

CHIH (not Chi)— Spelled this way, the word has many meanings. In T'ai Chi Chih, the Chih means "knowledge," or "knowing." In Chih-K'uan, which is the Chinese for the Indian "Samatha-Samapatti," it means "stoppage," with Chih-K'uan being "stopping and a view."

CHIH-K'UAN — A meditation of the Chinese T'ien T'ai Buddhists. First a "stopping" (fixation on a point of the body) and then a "view" (introspection of the thoughts).

CHING CHI SHEN — A popular Chinese spiritual expression, referring to "essence, intrinsic energy, spirit." In esoteric Taoism, it refers to the process of "mixing" by which the Immortal Spirit Body is cultivated.

CHUANG-TZU — One of the greatest Taoists and most famous philosophers of China, a follower of Lao-Tzu, who lived hundreds of years after the first master.

CHURCH OF WORLD MESSIANITY — The name given in English to the Japanese church "Sekai Kyu Seikyo," sometimes referred to as the "Healing Church" because of their healing practice of "Johrei."

COMPARATIVE MEDITATION — A term coined by the author for the courses (at university level and outside) where many mediation techniques are taught so the student can determine which is best for him, individually.

DARSHAN — In India it is felt that being in the presence of a saint, a God-man, brings great benefit, and this proximity is known as "Darshan."

DEVATA — A god, or aspect of Divinity. Indians usually have an "Ishta Devata," or aspect of the Supreme that they worship.

DEVI — Goddess. Many in India worship God in the aspect of Divine Mother.

DHARMAKARA — The name of Amida (Buddha of Infinite Light) aeons ago before he became a Buddha, at the time he took his 48 great vows.

DHARANI — The same as a Mantra, a formula or incantation of great power, referred to in Buddhism.

DHYANA — The Sanskrit word for meditation.

DUMO HEAT — The essence of Tibetan Buddhist practice, and also called the essence of "magic play," this great inner heat is cultivated by meditation practices. The "Dumo" is the same as "Tumo" in Chinese and, in China, it refers to the great meridian channel running down the front of the body.

ENERGY SEA — Around the T'an T'ien ("Tanden" in Japanese), the spot two inches below the navel, there is believed to be a great reservoir of intrinsic energy, the "Energy Sea" where the Chi is stored. It is from here that adepts in Karate and Aikido, bring the energy with a great shout when they smash their fists thru blocks of wood, or perform similar stunts.

EIGHT-FOLD PATH — The Buddha laid out a path of righteousness for those active in the world, including Right Livelihood and Right Concentration (meditation), with the seventh of the eight steps being "Right Mindfulness," practiced in the great Satipatthana meditation.

ETHERIC BODY — One of the sheaths referred to that is not the gross physical body. Some feel it is synonymous with the "astral body." There is no exact science for such terms.

FASTING MIND — Chuang-Tzu, the Chinese Philosopher, like his teacher, Lao-Tzu, suggested dropping things from the mind, not accumulating, thus returning to simplicity and spontaneity. This would be the "Fasting Mind." Buddhists might use the term differently, referring to the jettisoning of greed, anger, and delusion — the true fasting.

FIXATION — Anchoring the mind to one point in the body (usually the tip of the nose or spot two inches below the navel), as in Chih-K'uan practice.

GATE, GATE — The final words of the great Heart Sutra

(Hridaya) are felt to be an "unsurpassed Mantra," and they are "Gate Gate Paragate Parasamgate Godhi Svaha." Translations have been made, but they are unimportant, as there is really no translation for a Mantra.

GAUTAMA BUDDHA — "Gautama Siddhartha" was the name of a prince of the Sakyas in India. He renounced his princehood and became a wandering mendicant, reaching the great enlightenment that made him the Buddha, the "Perfected One."

GAYATRI — The name given to the sacred Mantra of the Vedas (original and most holy of Indian scriptures). High caste Brahmins use this Mantra at the investure of the Sacred Thread in the ceremony at puberty, but it is felt to be the one Mantra suitable for all Hindus. "Gayatri" has reference to the Divinity behind the Sun, much like Savitri.

GOHONZON — Mighty mysterious power of the universe as taught in Nichiren Buddhism of Japan (and Soka Gakai as well). This has to do with a Mandala — map of the universe — and is part of a mystic doctrine proclaimed by Nichiren.

GOLDEN FLOWER — The embryo of the Immortal Spirit Body as nurtured in Chinese esoteric Taoist practices. It is not "the light" that is circulated, as believed by some, but that which is nourished by the circulation of the light. *The Secret of the Golden Flower* is a famous book written about it.

GREAT CIRCLE MEDITATION — Name given by the author to the first part of the Reverse Meditative Breathings, corresponding to the "Macrocosmic Orbit."

GURU — Personal teacher in Indian (and Tibetan) tradition, supposedly a realized master in most cases.

HABIT ENERGIES — In Sanskrit these are known as

"Vashanas." They are the product of our habitual thinking, and literally make us what we will be in the future.

HAKUIN — The great 17th and 18th century Zen master in Japan, sometimes known as "Hakuin Zenji." One of the two most influential Zen teachers in Japanese history, the other being "Dogen Zenji."

HAM-SAH — In Indian Mythology, Hamsah is the Divine Swan. These two syllables are used, together, as a Mantra in India. It is interesting that the word "Hamsah" (perhaps spelled differently) is found as far away as the Sudan in Africa.

HANYA HARAMITA SHIN GYO — A Chinese transliteration of the Indian name, "Prajna-paramita." The great Heart Sutra ends with the expression "Maka Hanya Haramita Shin Gyo," meaning, literally "The Great Perfection of Wisdom." It is a Buddhist expression, and Prajnaparamita is often thought of as being female, the "mother," or "teacher," of all Buddhas.

HARE KRISHNA — An Indian cult that began several hundred years ago, when a modern Indian sage (Chaintanya) had revealed to him the great Mantra that goes: "Hare Krishna Hare Krishna Krishna Krishna Hare Hare — Hare Rama Hare Rama Rama Rama Hare Hare"

HATHA YOGA — Literally "Sun Moon" Yoga, "Ha" referring to the right eye, or sun, and "Tha" to the left eye, or moon. Thought of as the "Yoga of Physical Perfection," it is complete by itself, or the Asanas (postures) and other practices can be thought of as preliminaries in Rajah Yoga and Tantra.

HEART-FIRE — The physical heart is the great Yang (positive) in the body, and corresponds to the sun in the heavens. The Yang Chi (energy from the heart level) is to be brought down to the spot two inches below the navel, or to the soles of the feet, in T'ai Chi practice for healing purposes. The Chi of the great Yang, the heart, is thus the "Heart-Fire." Though he was not a Taoist, Hakuin Zenji, in his writings, stressed the efficacy of bringing the Heart-Fire down.

HEART SUTRA — By "heart" is meant "essence" or "gist." This short Sutra has the essence of the over 1700 Sutras (scriptures) called "Prajnaparamita" in Mahayana Buddhism.

HERPES SIMPLEX — A physical disorder that may afflict any part of the body, resulting in unpleasant blisters and discharge. It is often "brought on" by exposure to sunshine. From the author's point of view, this illustrates the heat element precipitating "purification."

HOLISTIC — (sometimes spelled "wholistic") The belief that man's body, mind, and spirit are one. "Holistic Medicine" attempts to treat physical ills thru this knowledge, not by just catering to physical symptoms. Many "Holistic Institutes" are springing up thruout the country; this is undoubtedly one direction the "healing arts" of the future will go.

HOUSEHOLDER — In India, where some renounce the world, there is also the majority that tends to marry, have children, and lead a worldly life. Actually, Indian scriptural teaching allows for both types of status in the course of a man's life, but such instructions are rarely followed in modern times. The "worldly man," who has a somewhat different and less stringent path to follow than the "renunciate," is called a "householder."

HRIDAYA — Literally means "heart" in Sanskrit, and is the true name of the Buddhist "Heart Sutra."

Glossary

I CHING — The great Chinese *Book of Changes*, which has influenced the whole growth of Chinese civilization, brings together the principles of Taoism and Confusianism. The "hexagrams" in the book are often used for divination, first thru the agency of yarrow stalks, and, today, by means of Chinese coins. The teaching of the *I Ching* emphasizes the cyclical principle of Yin-Yang philosophy, as opposed to ordinary causation. "There is a time to sow and a time to reap" would be a good example of this principle. There have been many famous commentaries on the *I Ching* (called "Wings"), the best-known coming from the Duke of Chou and the sage Confucius.

IDA, PINGALA — The major "nadis," or nerves, that run down the right and left sides of the body (criss-crossing) in Indian teaching. In the average man, the Prana (or Chi) flows thru these nadis, though, in the enlightened one, the Prana goes up the central channel, bringing great bliss.

INKA — Zen traces its history back to the Buddha himself, a 2500 year lineage in which masters who gave approval to enlightened disciples (some never had an enlightened disciple!) bestowed written approval called "Inka" on the fortunate ones, who were then free to teach and carry on the line of their master.

IMMORTAL SPIRIT BODY — Immortality while retaining the same individuality was the goal of esoteric Taoism. To reach this objective, practices were said to nourish an embryo (Golden Flower) that would mature as the "Immortal Spirit Body," a spiritual being within the physical body.

INTRINSIC ENERGY — Basically this refers to the Prana or Chi. It is also sometimes known as Kundalini or Shakti. There is controversy as to whether this is exactly the same as "vital force," but, for the practical purposes of meditative practice, they can be considered the same.

JAPA — Repetition of a Mantra (name of God, or aspect of God), whether that repetition be oral, mental, or written. Present-day teachers of India say that Japa (remembrance of the Name) is the best practice for this "degenerate" period of time known as the "Kali Yuga."

JHANNA — The Pali language word for "meditation," corresponding to the Sanskrit "Dhyana."

JOHREI — The act of focusing the hand on parts of the physical body by one trained to do so in the Japanese "Healing Church" known as Sekai Kyu Seikyo. A piece of paper worn in a locket around the neck, with the word "hikari," written on it by the religion's founder (Meishu Sama) or his descendant, is the "Sacred Focal Point" that gives power to the practice of Johrei. The word "hikari" means "light" in Japanese. Those receiving this Johrei often feel a strong heat, and the church reports many wonderful "cures," though it emphasizes it is raising the spiritual vibration with Johrei and not attempting to heal. This is an extremely interesting and, the author believes, efficacious way to use the Chi (Prana) to raise the body heat and bring about "purification."

KABIR — A Sufi Saint of the Middle Ages in India, a great poet who was expelled from the holy city of Benares. Though his devotional poetry is pure Sufi in content (the Sufis are called "The Mystic Arm of Islam"), Kabir was initiated and taught by a great Hindu guru.

KALI — One name given to "Divine Mother." The Ramakrishna Order, for instance, though part of Vedanta, worships "Mother" in many forms and under many names. Also known as "goddess Kali."

KALI YUGA — The "Iron Age." We are now in this supposedly degenerate age, the fourth Yuga in the incredibly long period of time known as "Kalpa," at the end of which the world is destroyed by flame, later to come back into being as the result of the unfulfilled desires expressed as habit energies (Vashanas), which lie dormant for awhile, and then spring to life again. Supposedly, we in this Yuga, live a shorter time than did those in previous divisions (Yugas) of this Kalpa.

KARMA — Literally "action." Every action must have a reaction. These reactions are "the fruits of Karma" and are the "fates" of individuals, brought about by their own actions. "As you sow, so shall you reap."

KEISAKU — The long stick carried by the monks who are patrolling the aisles during Zen Buddhist meditation (Zazen). They are usually empowered to use the sticks, not as punishment, but to "wake up" the one feeling the blows.

KENSHO — Literally, to "see the Buddha nature." In the West we hear much of Satori, the enlightenment experience, but Japanese Zen speaks more of "Kensho" which may be the result of many Satoris. To "rest in our own true nature" might roughly have the same meaning.

KOAN — The Japanese word for the Chinese "Kungan," literally a "case," that is, reference to an historical exchange, usually between master and disciple. The key part of such exchange forms an enigmatic problem on which many Zen monks (particularly those in "Rinzai Zen") ponder. Famous are such Koans as "If all things return to the One, to what does the One return?" The monk is expected to answer the Koan to the satisfaction of his master, and that does not necessarily mean an oral answer. Basically a Koan is a problem for meditation, the purpose of which is to encourage one-pointedness of mind.

KRISHNA — In India, Krishna is worshipped as an Avatar (incarnation in the body) of god Vishnu. Some worship Krishna, himself, as the Supreme. Everybody is familiar with the pictures of the beautiful boy Krishna playing his flute.

KRISHNAMURTI — A living writer who was born in India but raised in Europe by the Theosophic Society. Krishnamurti, a true spiritual iconoclast, has, thru his lectures and writings, shaken many people out of their accustomed way of thinking.

K'UAN — Literally, "a view." Though the word K'uan has many meanings in Chinese, here it refers to the second part of the Chih-K'uan meditation. In Sanskrit this is "Samatha Samapatti," referring to the two part practice of (1) concentrating intently on a spot in the body (usually the tip of the nose or the place two inches below the navel), and (2) introspecting the thoughts as they come. From a philosophic point of view there is a great deal more to K'uan, but, for meditation purposes, it is this introspection (watching) of the thoughts — which usually causes them to disappear so that one can return to the Chih part (the "fixation") of the meditation.

KUNDALINI — "Serpent" in Indian languages. It is said that there is a "sleeping serpent" of energy coiled at the base of the spine. In the advanced Yogi, this serpent uncoils and begins an ascent up the body, opening the power of the various psychic centers as it goes. The Kundalini is this latent power which can be aroused, and it has a good deal to do with sexual energy, as well as furnishing the power to progress toward enlightenment (liberation).

LEFT-HAND TANTRA — The "Tantras" are very old scriptures of India. When they were introduced into

Tibet, the Tantric beliefs combined with the Buddhism of the region to form the religion of "Tantric Buddhism," quite different from the "Tantric" faith of Northern India. There is an esoteric teaching in Tantric Buddhism which has to do with sexual activity (not true intercourse) as a means to enlightenment, performed under the guidance of a Lama (priest). This is a practice of the "Left-Hand Tantra," and is much misunderstood; most writers believe it stands for licentiousness. Therefore, the "left-hand" appellation is sometimes thought of as a term of derision.

LIKHITA JAPA — Repeating a Mantra by writing it (usually in a pattern), rather than uttering it.

LIN CHI — The Chinese name of the great Zen Master now known as "Rinzai" in Japan. It is the Rinzai Sect which primarily uses the Koan practice.

LOTUS — Here it refers to the "Lotus Posture," the way of cross-legged sitting in which the two feet are pulled up on the opposite thighs.

HALF-LOTUS — The sitting posture in which only one leg is pulled up on the opposite thigh.

LOTUS SUTRA — A great scripture of Buddhism. Coming from India, it became popular in China, and is felt to be THE key scripture by the Nichiren and Soka Gakai people of Japan. It is studied and honored by all Buddhists.

MACROCOSMIC ORBIT — The path from the top of the head down to the spot below the navel, then thru the legs and up the spine to the top of the head, as performed in "The Great Circle Meditation."

MAKYO — Illusory visions seen during Zen meditation practice.

MALA — A string of 108 beads used by Hindus as they perform Japa. Usually a devotee promises to repeat the name so many times during practice each day, and fingering the mala helps him keep count. There are rules as to how it is to be used.

MANASIKA JAPA — Japa is repetition of a Mantra, and Manasika Japa is performing the repetition mentally, making no sound. The popular "T.M." is really Manasika Japa.

MANDALA — A "Map of the Universe." Tibetans make many Mandalas, some very beautiful, and usually they have the figure of the Buddha (Vairocana Buddha), not the historical Buddha, in the center.

MANTRA — A word, or series of words of great power, revealed to an Indian sage during periods of austerity. The Mantra is a Name of God, or as aspect of God, and is not a sound made up by someone. Other countries also use Mantras ("Om Mani Padme Hum" being the great Tibetan Mantra), though they do not always call the Sacred Formula by the name "Mantra."

MILAREPA — Perhaps the greatest Tibetan Yogi, whose many spiritual poems are justly famous. He was an extreme ascetic in the latter part of his life, coming to Buddhism after having practiced "black magic" as a youth.

MUSHIN — "Mu" means "negative," and "Shin" means "mind," so this is translated as "no mind." It refers to the active mind not occupied with conceptual thinking, which corresponds to Chuang-Tzu's "fasting mind."

NADA — In Indian languages, this means "sound." "Nada Yoga" is an esoteric practice of "Sound Yoga." Actually, there is an involved metaphysics of sound in Indian philosophy, having to do with "Vak," "Para," and other vibrations, but "Nada" is a general word for sound. The Sikhs use the word "Shabd."

Glossary

NADIS — Unsatisfactorily translated as "nerves" or "nerve channels." There are numerous nadis in the body, and the Yogi often visualizes them around a psychic center (Chakra). The main ones, Ida and Pingala, carry the Prana and flow of breath for the average person; the advanced Yogi uses the thin central channel, the Sushumna, as well. These are all Nadis, and, in Hatha Yoga, there are eleborate means of purifying them.

NAMU AMIDA BUTSU — Called "Nembutsu," and it is like a Mantra. The Shin Buddhists of Japan repeat this formula endlessly, until it becomes part of them. The Nembutsu literally translates as "Hail to the Buddha of Infinite Light," and sincere repetition supposedly assures a devotee of being taken to the Pure Land, the Western Paradise, where conditions will be ideal for practice and attaining Nirvana.

NAMU MYO HO RENGE KYO — A formula (like a Mantra) of great power, taken from the "Lotus Sutra." Nichiren Buddhism followers use its repetition as their main practice, and many non-Buddhist religions in Japan also repeat this formula.

NEI KUNG — A secret meditation from China, performed while lying flat on the back. It has great healing power, and is known as "Nai Kan" in Japan, where it has almost disappeared.

NEMBUTSU — The "Namu Amida Butsu" explained above, a formula of great power.

NICHIREN — A controversial 12th Century saint in Japan, very bitter against foreigners and foreign imports. He had a running battle with Zen, the Japanese government, etc. There are many branches of Nichiren Buddhism in Japan, and the rapidly growing Soka Gakai religion might be thought of as one of them.

NIRVANA — Literally means "extinction" in Indian languages, but whether this is an actual blotting out (as thought by some primitive Buddhists), as extinction of the ego, or some other meaning, is not known. The Buddha did not define "Nirvana," but certainly it meant a status far beyond individuality, and it represents the ultimate goal of Buddhism. It was to be experienced, not talked about.

OBSESSION — The act of some non-embodied spirit taking over the body of a living person. To get rid of this spirit is the purpose of exorcism.

OM — Known as the "Pranava" in India, this is supposedly the first sound, the "word" from which all creation derives. It is much meditated on in India, but only a renunciate, not a worldly person, should do Japa (repetition) of this sacred sound, as it tends to lead one away from worldly life.

OM MANI PADME HUM — A sacred Mantra of Tibetan Tantric Buddhism. The words mean "The Gem in the Lotus," but the power of the Mantra goes far beyond semantic meanings.

ONE-POINTEDNESS — When the mind is occupied by only a single thought, steady in its absorption into that thought.

ORIGINAL FACE — A term used in Zen Buddhism, meaning your "True Self," or the essence of what you are far beyond individual personality. It has a universal connotation.

PATANJALI — Often called "The Father of Yoga." He did not invent it but codified and explained it in the great eight-part Rajah Yoga, on which he expounded in his "Yoga Sutras."

PARA — The Indians speak of vibration before sound, called "Para" (the term "Vak" is also used in slightly different connotation).

PRAJNA — A term used in Buddhism, where "Prajna" refers to the innate wisdom that has nothing to do with learning. "Prajnaparamita" would then be the "Perfection of Wisdom." In Yoga the steps to perfection end with "Samadhi," the superconsciousness state but, in Buddhism, the three steps are: conduct (Sila), concentration or meditation (Samadhi), and wisdom (Prajna), thus going one step beyond Yoga. The concept of "Prajna Wisdom" is very important in Zen practice.

PRANA — All the energy and force of the universe, is manifested in the individual as intrinsic energy. Kundalini and Shakti are manifestations of this universal energy. Chi is the Chinese name for Prana.

PRANAYAMA — One of the preliminary (outer) disciplines practiced in the eight-step Rajah Yoga. This is really the development of the Prana thru various breathing excercises. It is an involved art, usually mastered by Hatha Yoga adepts.

PUJA — A ceremony of dedication or devotion in India.

PURE LAND — Another name for the "Western Paradise," to which the faithful believer in the Amitabha Cult ("Amida" in Japan) will be taken by the Buddha of Infinite Light. More intellectual Buddhists, such as Zennists, believe the "Pure Land" is nothing else than the "Straightforward (or Pure) Mind."

RA — A seed syllable (Bija) having to do with the digestive fire and the psychic center associated with that part of the body. Used in Mantras such as Ram, short for Rama, in India. It is interesting that it was also the name of the sun god in Egyptian mythology, lending credence to its power as a fire aspect.

RAJAH YOGA — The "Kingly Yoga," Patanjali's great creation. It has eight steps: the first two, Yama and

Niyama, have to do with conduct and attitude. The next three are outer practices, that of posture (Asana), breathing excercises (Pranayama), and withdrawal of the senses from the field of the senses (Pratayahara). Finally, we have concentration, meditation, and Samadhi (culmination of deep meditation in the unshakable Super Conscious State). According to Patanjali, those who simply practice meditation, without the preliminaries, are doomed to disappointment.

RAMA — One of the greatest names in Indian Mythology, Rama (the hero of the great epic, "The Ramayana") was said to be an Avatar of Lord Vishnu, a divine incarnation here on earth. The name Rama is often repeated in Japa practice, and then it becomes Ram, one of the most popular Mantras in India.

RAMAKRISHNA — Living at the end of the nineteenth century, this renowned teacher of Vedanta is often referred to as one of the three great pillars of India, occurring at intervals of a thousand years (Buddha, Sankara, and Ramakrishna). This great teacher's disciple, Vivekananda, was largely responsible for popularizing Yoga in the West, and other disciples have spread Ramakrishna's teaching thruout the world. There are many "Maths" or "Ashrams" of Ramakrishna in the world today.

RAMANUJA — One of the greatest teachers of India, famed in the Middle Ages, he was the Guru of the poet Kabir, whom he initiated with the Mantra "Ram" that he was wont to use.

RENUNCIATE — One who renounces the world to follow austere spiritual practice. Such a one is usually called a sanyasin in India, though, actually, a Sanyasin is one who has been initiated into the Order of Sanyasa. "Swami" is another term that is often mistakenly applied to a renunciate. Such a one is not supposed to touch money, have possessions, etc. and is greatly respected, making it easy for him to live on alms.

REPS, PAUL — The name of a well-known living writer, whose book *Zen Flesh Zen Bones*, written in collaboration with the monk Sensaki, has become a classic in English.

RISHI (or RSHI) — A sage, usually out of India's history. Such a holy man, surprisingly, often was married and had a family. All true Mantras came thru such sages.

RINZAI — The Japanese name for the great Chinese Zen Master, Lin Chi. His own master was Huang Po, and he founded one of the five great divisions of Zen, only two of which flourish today (in Japan).

RINZAI ZEN — The Zen Buddhist sect in Japan that makes strong use of Koan practice, one of two sects that survive from the original five.

RAMANA MAHARSHI — A great sage of modern India, who died in recent times.

SADDAKA — One who follows a spiritual practice, or Sadhana. The term Saddhu means almost the same thing.

SAMADHI — When deep meditation becomes unshakable, it has reached Samadhi, the "super-conscious state." In Buddhism, Samadhi is also used in the sense of an enlightened state in which an adept continues thru the whole day, even while in activity.

SAMSKARA — Literally, "tendencies," though the word Samskara has other meanings. When habit energies go on for a long while, they may become tendencies (Samskaras) that carry over into subsequent lives.

SANKARA — (pronounced "Shankara") One of the greatest philosophers and holy men in India, called

Shankaracharya as a term of respect, "acharya" meaning "Great Master." A great advocate of Non-Dual Vedanta, he formed four outposts (north, south, east, and west) from which Pope-like teachers presided and went out to cater to spiritual needs. His writings and commentaries are the most famous in India, and yet he died a very young man.

SATORI — "Sudden enlightenment experience" in Zen, rather than a gradually developing state. It is taken from the Japanese verb "Satoru," meaning "to realize."

SATIPATTHANA — Literally, "The Way of Mindfulness," the Buddha's great meditation practice utilizing four "Ways of Mindfulness."

SEKAI KYU SEIKYO — The name of a Japanese religion with headquarters in Atami, Japan. Sometimes known as "The Healing Church," it makes great use of the healing practice called "Johrei." In the United States it is called "The Church of World Messianity."

SENNIN — Literally, "mountain hermit." There were legendary "Sennin" in Japan, and apparently, Hakuin Zenji met and was instructed by one named "Hakuyu," who was reputed to be several hundred years old.

SEVEN FACTORS OF ENLIGHTENMENT — The seven ingredients that the Buddha felt were necessary for enlightenment, "mindfulness" being the first of these.

SHAKTI — The female side, or consort, of Lord Shiva, Shiva is considered the immutable Reality, which becomes "Shakti," Power-Consciousness-Energy when he turns active and manifests as Universe. Shakti is worshipped by Tantriks, so, in a sense, this is "Energy-Worship." Prana and Chi ultimately have the same meaning as Shakti, without having the mythology attached to them.

SHAKYA — The tribe, or country, in which Gautama

Buddha was born. He was a prince of the Shakyas, destined to be their king until he left to become a wandering mendicant. As a result, the Buddha is often called Shakyamuni, "muni" meaning "a sage who teaches in silence." "Mowna" is "silence" in some Indian languages, and "muni" is associated with it, though most scholars ignore this fact and simply say that "muni" means "sage."

SASTRA — (pronounced "Shastra") A "doctrine," as in "Mantra Sastra," or the "Doctrine of Mantra Use."

SHIN — The word has many meanings in Chinese, often associated with "truth" or "heart." However, here it refers to the various sects of Amida Buddhism in Japan, including the best known, Jodo Shinshu.

SHINGON — Perhaps the first sect of Buddhism to arrive in Japan, it is derived from Tibetan practice and is often referred to as "Esoteric Buddhism." The pageantry and ceremony of Shingon appealed to nobility in Japan, and it was they, not the common people, who practiced Shingon. This sect still continues in Japan, but it is not as popular as it was in earlier days.

SHINSHU — A Japanese who practices a form of Buddhism is called "Shu" (as in Zen-shu), and "Shinshu" would be one practicing Shin Buddhism. However, the term is also used in respect to the Jodo Shinshu sect of Amida.

SHINTO — Not really a religion, Shinto is a "nature way" that is followed by all Japanese, of whatever denomination. Supposedly every male Japanese makes a pilgrimage to Ise, most holy of Shinto shrines. There are innumerable Shinto gods, and these were brought into the Buddhist pantheon when Buddhism began to grow popular in Japan. Shinto is really an extraordinary way of some beauty, and well worth studying by itself.

Glossary

SHIVA — The "Destroyer" aspect of the trio of gods, Brahma, Vishnu, and Shiva. However, some in India also worship Shiva as the sole ultimate Divinity or Reality. Such worshippers are called "Shaivites."

SUNYATA — (pronounced Shunyata) The Buddhist term for "void" or "emptiness," though this emptiness does not imply lack of anything — it contains all manifestations, or transformations, within it. The "empty" part means "empty of enduring Self-Nature." The study of Shunyata is absolutely essential for anyone who would understand Buddhism, particularly Mahayana (or "greater vehicle") Buddhism.

SIDDHI — The great power attained by advanced Yogis, seemingly supernatural to those who do not understand their basis.

SO'HAM — A famous Mantra that means "That I Am." In this book it is used in the practice co-ordinating the Mantra with the breath, and this practice is reputed to bring Siddhis (powers) to those who use it faithfully.

SOKA GAKAI — A recently arisen sect of Buddhism that follows many of the teachings of Nichiren. Soka Gakai has a strong political arm and is thought not to be true Buddhism by many scholars in and of Japan.

SOUL TRAVEL — Some groups teach a form of astral travel that is highly dangerous, and this is called "Soul Travel."

ST. JOHN OF THE CROSS — A great Christian mystic, who left many fine writings.

SUFI — Though the Sufis (literally "wool-clad") are known as the Mystics of Islam, they claim Sufism is a substratum of all religions and spiritual practices. The great Sufi poets, such as Rumi and Omar Khayam, are well-known in the West.

SUSHUMNA — The thin thread-like channel that goes up the center of the body, not open to the average man, but available to the adept, and responsible for great Bliss as the Prana ascends in the body. One of the Nadis.

SUTRA — In Buddhism, a Sutra is a teaching spoken personally by the Buddha. However, other Sutras in India, not Buddhist, are usually made up of groups of succinct aphorisms.

SWAMI RAMDAS — One of the most beloved of modern Indian saints, known for his devotion to Ram (aspect of God). He died in recent years.

T'AI CHI CHIH — A series of twenty separate movements that strongly circulates the Chi. Based on ancient principles, it was developed by the author and first taught in 1974.

T'AI CHI CH'UAN — First of the Martial Arts, formerly called "Shadow-Boxing." Over a thousand years old in China, such disciplines as Karate and Aikido are thought to be derived from it. The classical form is a long "dance" of 108 movements, a true Moving Meditation.

T'AI CHI GIK — A legendary form of self-defense, in which the practicer could supposedly paralyze an adversary by touching him relative to the time of day, season of the year, etc. (each indicating where the Chi would be flowing most strongly in the body). It is said that the form was legally abolished because of injuries and fatalities occurring from its practice. The author believes he met the last, or one of the last, of its masters in Taiwan some years ago.

T'AI CHI — Supreme Ultimate; a synonym of Tao.

TAKA AMAHARA — A poem or chant used by the Church of World Messianity, this is really a Shinto prayer to various Shinto gods. Said to have a very high vibration.

TAN T'IEN — (pronounced "dantienne") The spot two inches below the navel, the "field of the Tan elixir."

TANTRIC BUDDHISM — Tibetan Buddhism, representing a combination of Tantric teachings (of North India) and Mahayana Buddhism.

TANTRIKS — Followers of the Tantric faith of India. Sometimes Tantric Buddhists are also called "Tantriks."

TAKUSAN — (also spelled "Tokusan") Japanese pronunciation of a famous Chinese Zen master's name.

TANDEN — The Japanese word for "Tan T'ien," the spot below the navel.

TAO — Chinese word for Reality, seen by Chinese sages as a "moving force," a flowing stream with which we should accord, often called "Supreme Ultimate." The scholar, Wen-Shan Huang, has likened Tao to the Western concept of Mana. "Taoism" is a philosophy that became a Religion — based on the concept of the all-embracing Tao.

TATHAGATA — A term applied to the Buddha, literally meaning "He who has thus come." Tathagata and Buddha are interchangeable.

TOXIN — The "Healing Church," Sekai Kyu Seikyo, uses this word to describe the impurities that are physical in nature but have spiritual derivation. The purpose of "Johrei" practice is to purify the body of these "toxins," accumulated for long periods of time.

TUMO — (pronounced dumo) The major front meridian channel. It is important in acupuncture, and in such practices as T'ai Chi Chih.

TURIYA STATE — The "Fourth State of Consciousness" that underlies the ordinary waking, sleeping, and dream states. While these latter three are constantly changing, the "Reality," or Turiya State, is unchanging. When deep meditation goes beyond thought, the meditator has entered the Turiya State.

UDIYANA — One of the Asanas, or postures, of Hatha Yoga. Quite advanced, it has another form called "Naoli," and is very difficult to do.

VAIKHARI JAPA — Oral repetition of a Mantra, usually performed while holding the string of 108 beads known as a Mala.

VASHANA — Habit energy. When we repeat a thought or action so often it mentally becomes a compelling force, that is a Vashana.

VIPASSYANA — Literally, "insight." In Buddhism, there are short (ten days or two weeks) meditation retreats, which often bring about an "insight experience," almost a minor Satori. However, often the meditator is not ready for the forced experience and it fades. The "Burmese Method" taught in Burma, India, and Ceylon refers to Vipassyana practice.

VISHNU — One of the trilogy of main Indian gods, Vishnu represents the Sustaining Force (Brahma is the Creator, and Shiva the Destroyer). Some in India worship Vishnu as the sole Divinity, however.

VITAL FORCE — The Chi or Prana.

VRITTI — The groove in the brain made by thought or reaction, according to Indian belief. Each idea supposedly makes a sound, which creates the groove known as Vritti (explaining memory). When a Vritti is continually being made, thru repetition, it may ripen into a Vashana, or habit energy.

WESTERN PARADISE — The "Pure Land" to which sincere believers in Amida Buddha go.

YAHOO — A sound used by the Sufis, almost like a

Mantra, supposedly to eventually result in illumination when properly uttered.

YIN-YANG — Juxtoposition of the negative and positive. All Chinese cosmology is based on the interplay of these two types of energy, and the Moving Meditations attain their great benefits thru balancing of the circulated Yin-Yang energies. It is said by some scholars that the development of the computer was largely due to the Yin-Yang theory.

ZAZEN — The term for Zen "sitting." While it is a posture for Zen meditation, Zen teachers insist one can be doing "Zazen" while brushing the teeth or performing labor if the mind is properly controlled.

HEALING THRU JOY!

Justin Stone
A.S.C.A.P.

Joy,   Joy,   Heal-ing thru Joy!   Joy,   Joy,   Heal-ing thru Joy!

Joy in the Heart!   Joy in the Mind!   Joy in the Soul!   Joy,   Joy,

Heal-ing thru Joy!   Joy,   Joy,   Heal-ing thru Joy!

One with all   Life,
One with the   Earth,
Free as the   Breeze,

Happ-y am   I!   One with all   Life,   Heal-thy am   I!   One with all   Life,
Joy-ous am   I!   One with the   Sun,   Joy-ous am   I!   One with the   Sky,
Joy-ous am   I!   Free as the   Clouds,   Joy-ous am   I!   Right as the   Rain,

Hol- y am   I!   Joy,   Joy,   Heal- ing with   Joy!
Joy-ous am   I!
Joy-ous am   I!

For a complete catalog of books and tapes by Justin F. Stone and other authors, please contact the publisher:

Good Karma Publishing, Inc.
P.O. Box 511
Fort Yates, ND 58538
Phone - 701/854-7459 or toll-free - 888/540-7459
Fax - 701/854-2004